CONDUCTING PRACTITIONER RESEARCH IN PHYSICAL EDUCATION AND YOUTH SPORT

There is now a widespread expectation that teachers and coaches should be reflective practitioners, an expectation written into national standards of education in many countries. This innovative book introduces methods by which teachers and coaches can conduct research into their own professional practice and therefore become more effective reflective practitioners, improving their students' learning as a result.

As the only book on practitioner research that focuses specifically on the unique challenges of working in a physical education or youth sport environment, it uses real-life case studies and applied practical examples to guide the reader through the research process step by step. Examining the what, why and how of four key research methods in particular – action research, narrative inquiry, autoethnography and self-study – it provides an expert analysis of the strengths and limitations of each method and demonstrates how conducting reflective research can produce tangible results in improving both teaching and learning.

This is an invaluable resource for all those interested in enhancing their professional development as students, practitioners or researchers of physical education and youth sport.

Ashley Casey is a Senior Lecturer in Pedagogy at Loughborough University, UK.

Tim Fletcher is an Associate Professor in Physical Education at Brock University, Canada.

Lee Schaefer is an Assistant Professor in the Department of Kinesiology and Physical Education at McGill University, Canada.

Doug Gleddie is Associate Professor in the Department of Elementary Education at the University of Alberta, Canada.

CONDUCTING PRACTITIONER RESEARCH IN PHYSICAL EDUCATION AND YOUTH SPORT

Reflecting on Practice

Ashley Casey, Tim Fletcher, Lee Schaefer and Doug Gleddie

Routledge
Taylor & Francis Group

LONDON AND NEW YORK

First published 2018
by Routledge
2 Park Square, Milton Park, Abingdon, Oxon OX14 4RN

and by Routledge
711 Third Avenue, New York, NY 10017

Routledge is an imprint of the Taylor & Francis Group, an informa business

© 2018 Ashley Casey, Tim Fletcher, Lee Schaefer and Doug Gleddie

British Library Cataloguing-in-Publication Data
A catalogue record for this book is available from the British Library

Library of Congress Cataloging-in-Publication Data
A catalog record for this book has been requested

ISBN: 978-1-138-89218-7 (hbk)
ISBN: 978-1-138-89219-4 (pbk)
ISBN: 978-1-315-70928-4 (ebk)

Typeset in Bembo
by Apex CoVantage, LLC

Ash: Sarah, who always believes in me. Thomas, who pops, double taps, aerials and trades like no one else. Maddie, who always makes me laugh and emojis me. I love you all.

Tim: My sister, Jacqui. For past and future conversations serious and light, personal and professional. With hopes that the book captures a fraction of the purpose and commitment you bring for your students.

Lee: Everlee, Cove, Bryar, and my teammate Laura, who remind me on a daily basis that although I love my work, it is only a fraction of my life.

Doug: Jodi, Elia, Meaghan and all the other MEd students who have embraced reflective practice. You inspire and remind me of what it takes to be a master teacher.

From all of us: To the students, staff, colleagues, mentors, mentees, peers, friends and families who have helped us and put up with our crazy ideas − too many to mention here and stay within the word count − we offer up our thanks and gratitude. A bit of each of you is in this book − and no, you can't have it back. We'd specifically like to thank Jo Bailey, Jodi Harding-Kuriger, Brian Lewis and Ciara Griffin for lending their voices and experiences to this book. We literally couldn't have done this without you. To the reviewers of our proposal, and to Simon Whitmore, Cecily Davey and all at Routledge − thanks for seeing something in our idea for a book. Thanks also go to Kathy Armour for taking the time to read the book, comment on it and, unsurprisingly, for challenging us to take our ideas forwards. Finally, to the practitioners we hope find use and inspiration in this book − your commitment to what you do continues to inspire us.

CONTENTS

viii Contents

8 Using autoethnography to explore a culture of school sport 95

9 Using self-study of practice to examine pedagogies that
    promote meaningful participation 109

PART IV **119**

10 Acknowledging bias 121

11 Ethical responsibilities of being a practitioner researcher 129

12 Aligning beliefs and actions 139

PART V **147**

13 Overview of practitioner research 149

Index 159

FIGURES AND TABLES

Figures

Tables

PREFACE

In the time we've known each other we've never all been in the same geographical location at the same time. We met through acquaintances, and then 'met' through digital media. That's not to say we haven't met under various guises and at different conferences. Tim, Doug and Lee meet regularly on the Canadian circuit but Ash has not been at those conferences. Ash and Tim met at the American Educational Research Association's (AERA) annual meeting in New Orleans in 2010, and again in Vancouver in 2012 and Philadelphia in 2014. Lee was at the Philadelphia meeting, but Doug wasn't. Ash met Lee again at the International Association for Physical Education in Higher Education congress in Madrid in 2015. Doug was there too, but Tim wasn't.

Despite never meeting as a collective, we have worked together on several projects, and these have been driven by a desire to improve and enhance practice – both our own and that of others. And that desire is really what is at the heart of this book. We came together because of a shared sense of frustration about practitioner research in physical education and coaching. We had all worked with large numbers of practitioners – both practicing and aspiring – and been faced with similar assumptions:

- 'Action research is just research done by people on themselves.'
- 'Narrative inquiry is about writing stories isn't it?'
- 'Isn't autoethnography just writing about yourself?'
- 'I'm not a teacher educator, so I can't do self-study, can I?'

And we have all been asked a variety of questions:

- 'How do I improve my coaching/teaching practice?'
- 'Why should I bother reflecting on my practice?'
- 'What strategies are effective for reflecting?'

Over the years we realised that while we'd all developed different responses to the assumptions underlying these questions, our respective answers had a commonality and shared purpose. What we also realised was that we shared a lot of common ground and could help one another to better understand the landscape and practices we found ourselves in and among. Most importantly, though, we also realised that we hadn't written any of this stuff down and couldn't go to a single source to help others who were looking for their own answers. So we decided to write this book.

We are grateful to Routledge for sharing the vision we had for a book on practitioner research and the academics and teachers who reviewed our proposal and helped to make it better. We are particularly grateful to the four practitioners who worked with us and to one another for creating a challenging and yet rewarding space in which to have these discussions. We didn't agree on everything and we hope the book you're about to read reflects this. We knocked down a few doors and broke a few gazebos in our quest to make this book work in a way that would be helpful, useable and challenging for you – we hope! We've learned a lot. So even if no one buys the book we're OK with that. However, we do sincerely hope that this is a work that helps teachers and aspiring teachers, coaches and aspiring coaches to develop their pedagogies by researching themselves and finding their own answers.

Ash, Tim, Lee and Doug
Spring 2017

FOREWORD

This is a research methods book with a difference. It is focused on the what, the why and – in particular – the how of four research methods: action research, narrative inquiry, autoethnography and self-study. These four methods have a distinguished history in the fields of education, physical education and coaching. Nonetheless, these and other methods located at the so called 'soft' end of science are often marginalised. One reason may be that instead of providing certainties, these methods tend to deliver outcomes that are complex, detailed, insightful and even puzzling. Indeed, it is surely impossible to engage in the level of detail and critical reflection that these methods require and then produce simplicity and certainty. Moreover, this book has been written primarily for practitioners and if there is one thing that an experienced practitioner knows, it is that practice in physical education and sport is rarely simple. So, in this book we have something that embraces complexity instead of attempting to edit it out.

The lead authors have written this book in collaboration with each other and with practitioners. Their aim was to contribute to the enhancement of their own practice and also that of teachers and coaches. To do this, Ash, Lee, Doug and Tim have constructed a book that is onion-like in its layers. Born of frustration with much work on practitioner research, they have developed an approach that moves from an overview of the theory and existing research in each of the four main research methods, to a description and analysis of practitioners using each of these methods, to a Socratic-like conversation between the four authors on the issues that arose.

In Part II, the chapters provide an overview of each of the methods – action research, narrative inquiry, autoethnography and self-study – making this the most traditional section of the book (alongside the introduction and conclusion in Parts I and V, respectively). Readers can use this background material to ensure they have sufficient understanding of the range, strengths and limitations of each method. As is noted in Chapter 3 on narrative inquiry, there is research methods literature available, but very little makes it accessible to practitioners in ways that are useful. In Chapter 4 on autoethnography this point is made even more forcefully, describing much of the available research as 'Highly theoretical, full of big words and jargon, not to mention being published in journals that are expensive and inaccessible to most teachers and coaches.' I made similar points in my recent work on pedagogical cases (*Pedagogical Cases in Physical Education and Youth Sport*, Routledge, 2014).

Part III takes the analysis to a different level. True to the ambition to offer a better way to support and engage practitioners, each chapter provides detailed information on the process of conducting practitioner enquiry and what can be learned from it. Inevitably, we find that the practitioners are drawn into the complexity and nuance of each research process and as they develop new insights, so does the reader. It is also worth noting that although each of these chapters set out to focus on a different method, each has ended up as an amalgam of action, narrative, and self reflection; in other words, the methods merge in interesting ways. This aspect of the work could be taken further in the future.

In Part IV, the authors attempt something different. In reflecting on the lessons learned from completing the chapters in Parts II and III, they identified three recurring cross-chapter issues that require deeper analysis: handling bias, conducting ethical research, and aligning beliefs with actions in practice. They have chosen to present these issues in the form of academic conversations between the four authors, adding another layer of analysis and insight. I anticipate that this part will be of particular interest to researchers and students, while Parts II and III will meet the immediate needs of practitioners. In summary, the authors have achieved their aim of offering something new and different to support the professional development of practitioners and researchers working in physical education and sport.

Professor Kathy Armour
Pro-Vice-Chancellor (Education)
University of Birmingham
June 2017

PART I

1

TAKING PRACTITIONER RESEARCH ONTO THE FIELD

Introduction

Don't get lost. Give it a try. Go find the place that you're wishing for.

Natsuki Takaya (creator of *Fruits Basket* manga series)

The drive in modern life is around improvement. Nothing, it seems, is ever right. Governments are elected on promises to make things better. We are bombarded with myriad social initiatives, while on a personal level there are countless self-help books or personal development courses which promise that things can and will get better. The internal and external pressures to improve often contain very practical implications because we are typically judged – both professional and personally – on that improvement. And yet, while a lot of the resources (both human and material) that encourage us to improve tell us what we can improve and why improving in one or more areas of our lives might be important, we feel that they often fall short of helping us understand *how* to improve.

Teaching and coaching are no different. Pedagogues are banded by their experiences and castigated for their 'wet behind the eared' naivety or 'stuck in their ways' dogmatism. And both are told to change. Veterans and newbies alike are asked to change, to improve and grow but aren't, in our experiences, given the tools to make such a metamorphosis. We've been there, done that and bought several T-shirts (and books) that promised the world and failed to deliver. And thus, the rusty wheel turns and the cycle of dogmatism endures. We are judged by other people's standards and forget, sometimes, to apply our own. Practitioners often have a wealth of knowledge of their craft, the people with whom they are working, and the contexts in which that work takes place. How such knowledge is developed and how it can be expanded or deepened remains somewhat mysterious, at least to many teachers and coaches. That's not to say that we have *the* solution and have written it all down. This is not our purpose in writing this book. Instead, we hope/aspire/desire to provide some examples, ideas and tools that have worked for us.

Changing behaviour, and in turn professional practice, is not something we can do on request, at least not in meaningful and enduring ways. There are myths that would lead us to believe that the initial steps in change are relatively straight-forward: we decide to change, we become educated about the change, we have the skills to change, and *hey presto!* We make a change. However, we know that change is much more complex and difficult than these myths would lead us to believe (Kelly & Barker, 2016). And if it is difficult to begin to make a change, it is similarly difficult to change professional practice in the long-term. As Goodyear and Casey (2015) explain, the difficulty comes in sustaining that change beyond the honeymoon period of innovation. This often requires a shift in thinking, moving beyond the sense of celebration and emancipation and settling in a space where the new becomes the established form of practice. In embracing the new, the practitioner must make herself or himself comfortable with discomfort, and understand that confusion, uncertainty and doubt are to be embraced. Many might argue this goes against human nature, as it seems our mission is often to seek comfort and routine. Williams (1977) suggests that emerging belief and action is highly influenced by our dominant and residual beliefs and actions. He argues that in seeking a change in ideology and practice we must reposition ourselves to make the emergent and the new our dominant way of thinking, saying and doing (Kemmis & Grootenboer, 2008). However, even if we manage this, our once dominant beliefs lurk in the dark corners of our practice, to 'ambush' us in our most challenging and difficult moments. Perhaps even to save us from the moment. But in saving us, and in working in that moment, we are drawn back to our past practices (the ones we wanted to change) and thus engage in what Evans (1985) called 'innovation without change'.

If our aim is to avoid the status quo, and if our ambition is to break the hold of our dominant practices, then we need to better understand the world in which we live. That is not to say we need to better understand *the* world itself but that we need to understand *our* world. John Dewey describes this as a pragmatic ontology and suggests that this characterises reality as living within an individual's experiences. In other words, 'what you see (and hear, feel, think, love, taste, despise, fear, etc.) is what you get. That is all we ultimately have in which to ground our understanding. And that is all we need' (Clandinin & Rosiek, 2007, p. 41).

To see reality as living in our experiences we must seek to understand those experiences. We need to be able to unpack what we see, feel, hear, etc. and we need tools that help us to do that. This is what practitioner research allows us to do. It allows us to experience the village of our lives rather than the cities and continents of our world. In doing so we can effect change in our emerging, dominant and residual practices. And perhaps the village can begin to change the world.

The village

> Too much research is published to the world and not enough to the village.
>
> (Stenhouse, 1981, p. 111)

In his conceptualisation of the teacher-as-researcher, Lawrence Stenhouse envisioned, we believe, someone who could talk the local dialect, who understood the local customs and who could effect change that was meaningful to the local community. In arguing that, as researchers, we seek a global audience he was also remonstrating with us for not looking to the everyday activities of teachers (and coaches). Yet he also aspired for more. He was interested in helping pedagogues to push back against the never ceasing tide of theory and policy that pervade their lives almost daily and to apply experienced practical judgement to the plethora of 'good ideas' they are obliged to receive. He saw the classroom not just as a place to test theory – although this was one of his key messages – but also as a place of 'intellectual innovation which brings in its trail a press towards social change' (Stenhouse, 1981, p. 103).

Donald Schön (1983) similarly argued that teachers should be reconceptualized as researchers. In particular, Schön described how reflection in-action (professional knowledge used to make decisions from moment to moment) and reflection on-action (professional knowledge used to analyse past experiences to decide how to adapt for the future) represent the distinct, often tacit forms of knowledge possessed by teachers and other professionals. One of the main difficulties, however, lies in the ways professionals can make their tacit knowledge of practice explicit, so that they and others might benefit. In this way, we think, both Stenhouse and Schön aspired not only for researchers to talk to the metaphorical village, but for the village to talk to researchers and to share these conversation with the wider world.

Unfortunately, these conversations are nowhere near as common as they could be. Indeed, as we have argued elsewhere, the public reflections of teachers (or indeed the reflective teacher) are more 'the talked about' than the 'actioned' realities of education (Casey, 2013). This dearth of interaction and understanding around schools (and clubs) as individual rather than collective institutions may be as much to do with the fact that the process of self-enlightenment is not traditionally part of a practitioner's habitual practice. Yet, as Brookfield (1995) warns, innocence is believing that we fully understand what we are doing and how we are affecting learners. Only by answering the urge to change practice, to understand practice, and challenge the conditions of practice (Kemmis, 2009) can we truly be said to understand 'how to go on' in practice (ibid., p. 467).

The assumed ignorance of the village and its inhabitants

> A tendency among researchers is to ask questions about issues that they could antici-
> pate to be too difficult to answer to both teachers and pupils, particularly uses about
> important knowledge and learning – and then be critical about the poor quality of
> the answers.
>
> (Larsson & Redelius, 2004, p. 394)

Anthropologists seek to explore local cultures without, in any way, attempting to change those local cultures. Yet one of the criticisms of anthropology has been the incredible difficulty of that very objective. By being in a position to observe behaviour and custom, some have argued that outsiders run the risk of changing the very thing they came to see (this is known as the Hawthorne effect: see McCambridge, Witton & Elbourne, 2014). Early missionaries, on the other hand, were overt in their desire to change what they deemed as ignorance and install their own practices and beliefs in place of the customs and traditions they found on arrival. Do researchers – in asking deliberately difficult questions and then offering criticism of practitioners' limited responses – run the risk of running roughshod over the behaviours and good practices of the very people they come to engage with? How could an outsider possibly know more about the complex contexts, relationships and lived curriculum than the person in the midst of all of this?

Armour (2006) writes of the unheard and under-represented nature of teachers' lives and asks that, as researchers, we take the time to help them to articulate their experiences or those of their peers. And yet we know that teachers and coaches and other practitioners articulate their experiences with their peers constantly. So perhaps Armour is hoping that researchers may value practitioners' lives enough to actually listen to what they have to say, and help to include their lives in research texts.

In a similar way to Armour (ibid.), Connelly and Clandinin (1988, 1990) suggested that teachers lead storied lives and that often these stories are discounted by researchers who position themselves as experts attempting to fix teachers up. Clandinin and Connelly's (2000) commitment to better understanding teachers' stories, and in turn their experiences, positioned researchers and practitioners on a level playing field. They stated: 'when both researchers and practitioners tell stories of the research relationship, they have the possibility of being stories of empowerment' (Connelly & Clandinin, 1990, p. 4).

The positioning of the teacher-as-researcher by Stenhouse, Schön, Clandinin and Connelly, as pioneers in the field of education, will be exemplified in this book. Yet we also hope to show that the busyness inherent in teaching and coaching means that it is impossible to deny the difference between what practitioners feel they could achieve and what they actually 'pull off' (Lawson, 1993). As a consequence, teachers and coaches adopt what Sparkes (1988) called 'micropolitical strategies' when it comes to surviving and thriving at work. Yet this 'wheeling and dealing' (ibid., p. 157) in the 'arenas of struggle' that are professional knowledge landscapes are unlikely to be shared with outsiders. Practitioner research allows us to see into the microcosms of schools and sports clubs and better understand what actually happens there. It also allows us to move beyond the idea that teachers and coaches are limited in their understanding and stops researchers resorting to criticism as their first response to apparently unchanging practices and to what they see as ignorance (Larsson & Redelius, 2004).

Practitioner research

The term *reflective practitioner* has become the 'watchword' for the twenty-first-century pedagogue yet it has been described as a 'talked about' rather than an 'actioned' notion of the professional practitioner (Casey, 2013). That said, because of the rise in the perceived importance of reflective practice and the expectations of practitioners to engage in such endeavours, practitioner research is a growing field of study in physical education and youth sport (Tinning, 2014). However, the multiple ways of doing practitioner research – of which the specifics are often unfamiliar to teachers, coaches, and teacher/coach educators alike – often results in a gestalt form of personal inquiry. This gestalt borrows the most convenient parts of different approaches while failing to consider the epistemological and ontological obligations as well as the practical work that has occurred over generations to refine and develop each approach.

Cochran-Smith and Lytle (2007, p. 25) described the term *practitioner research* as 'a conceptual and linguistic umbrella to refer to a wide array of education research modes, forms, genres, and purposes.' They argue that the expression encompasses a range of educational research methodologies and methods including but not limited to: action research; teacher research; self-study; narrative (or autobiographical) inquiry; the scholarship of teaching and learning; and the use of teaching as a context for research (ibid., p. 25). It is useful here to explore their definitions of each of these genres further before explaining how the selection that we included in this book are relevant:

> **Action research**: a methodology commonly used in collaborations between teachers and university-based researchers for the alteration of curriculum and common practices in schools through problem-posing, data collection, analysis and action.
>
> **Teacher research**: a term which refers to the increase in teacher inquiry in North America in the 1980s.
>
> **Self-study**: the personal studies of teacher educators in higher education.
>
> **Narrative inquiry (or autobiographical inquiry)**: refers to the knowledge-bearing stories written by teachers following systematic reflections around their biographies and experiences of school and teaching.
>
> **The scholarship of teaching and learning**: the studying, understanding, and enhancement of teaching and learning in primary and secondary schools and universities.
>
> **The use of teaching as a context for research**: the trend for researchers to adopt the role of teacher in an effort to understand the complexities and problems of teaching.
>
> *(Adapted from Cochran-Smith & Lytle, 2007, pp. 25–26)*

In grouping these six genres of research, Cochran-Smith and Lytle (2007) went on to justify their choices by exploring the shared features that cut across all. The primary aspect of all forms of practitioner research, they said, is the notion that the practitioner himself or herself takes on the role of researcher. Secondly, practitioner research works on the premise that, in order to comprehend and therefore improve practice, the interplay of power relationships and the workplace has to be expressly understood in the context of daily work. Finally, the very same professional context is the site of any practitioner inquiry and the 'problems and issues that arise from professional practice are taken up as topics of study' (ibid., p. 26).

Despite the plethora of practitioner research approaches shown above we decided to choose three from Cochran-Smith and Lytle's (2007) list: action research, narrative inquiry and self-study. We then added autoethnography because of its features that allow for a rich exploration of the self in cultural contexts. We have done this not in an effort to devalue the other approaches we chose not to include, but to acknowledge our own experiences and respective expertise. Fundamentally, we wanted to write a book steeped in our own experiences and informed by our own practices. As such, Ash has written about action research as it underpinned his own journey from teacher-as-teller to teacher-as-facilitator. Lee explores autobiographical narrative inquiry because he has used this extensively to study his own practice, as well as to study the experiences of early career physical educators and teachers. Doug looks at autoethnography because he has been using autoethnography in his own reflective practice, research and with graduate students. Finally, Tim explores self-study because he uses self-study of professional practice to examine the work he does as a teacher educator, and shares his insights and understandings with members of that community of researchers.

What to expect from the book

Drawing on our experiences as four practitioner researchers – all with a different specialism – we take the time to explore the distinct features of four widely accepted approaches to practitioner research: action research, narrative inquiry autoethnography, and self-study of practice. Following this introductory chapter, the second part of the book (i.e. the next four chapters) includes the theoretical underpinnings, affinities, differences, and possibilities of each of the chosen approaches and considers the implications for both research and pedagogy. This is not to say that each methodology requires teachers or coaches to work alone, but rather it respects the identities and contextual uniqueness of the personal and professional lives of the practitioners engaged in this type of work, and is focused on how practitioner researchers make sense of their own lived experience. Thus, these four approaches allow the practitioner researcher to conduct rigorous research (that is, there are standards or steps to ensure quality and trustworthiness) that also attends to the practitioner researcher's unique situation, set of circumstances and experiences. Along with the philosophical ideals of the four methodologies we discuss, there is also a pragmatic reason for our selection. The four methodologies we include in this book position the practitioner themselves as the main data gathering instrument: this means that the practitioner researcher themselves is the primary tool used to conceptualise the research, gather data, perform the analyses, and interpret the findings so they have application and relevance for the context in which they are working.

In an attempt to integrate theory and practice, we invited four practitioners (Jo Bailey, Jodi Harding-Kuriger, Brian Lewis and Ciara Griffin) to co-author chapters with us in Part III of the book. These four chapters are examples of how Jo and Ash, Jodi and Doug, Brian and Lee, and Ciara and Tim used action research, narrative inquiry, autoethnography and self-study of practice respectively to inquire into practice and deepen understanding of teaching and learning in physical education and youth sport. We felt it was important to showcase examples of practitioners working alongside researchers, actively inquiring together to help bridge the gap that is so often evident; a point we explained earlier in this chapter.

In the fourth part of the book we present three common issues faced by practitioner researchers, and share our thoughts on how someone using each methodology would approach or consider those issues. In this part, we structure the chapters differently than in the first three sections. We provide the text from fairly candid and unpolished conversations we had with one another, both hearing and presenting different perspectives and identifying common ground.

The final part consists of one chapter, where we try to identify common threads, key insights and significant perspectives that we hope readers take away from the book, and can apply to their professional practice and ongoing learning.

References

Armour, K. (2006). Physical education teachers as career-long learners: A compelling research agenda. *Physical Education & Sport Pedagogy, 11*(3), 203–207.

Brookfield, S. (1995). *Becoming a critically reflective teacher.* San Francisco, CA: Jossey Bass.

Casey, A. (2013). Practitioner research: A means of coping with the systemic demands for continual professional development? *European Physical Education Review, 19*, 76–90.

Clandinin, D.J., & Connelly, F.M. (2000). *Narrative inquiry: Experience and story in qualitative research.* San Francisco: Jossey-Bass.

Clandinin, D.J., & Rosiek, J. (2007). Mapping a landscape of narrative inquiry: borderland spaces and tensions. In D.J. Clandinin (ed.), *Handbook of narrative inquiry: Mapping methodology* (pp. 35–75). Thousand Oaks, CA: Sage.

Cochran-Smith, M., & Lytle, S.L. (2007). Everything's ethics. In A. Campbell & S. Groundwater-Smith (eds), *An ethical approach to practitioner research: Dealing with issues and dilemmas in action research* (pp. 24–41). London: Routledge.

Connelly, F.M., & Clandinin, D.J. (1990). Stories of experience and narrative inquiry. *Educational Researcher, 19*(5), 2–14.

Connelly, F.M., & Clandinin, D.J. (1988). *Teachers as curriculum planners: Narratives of experience.* New York: Teachers College Press.

Evans, J. (1985). *Teaching in transition: The challenge of mixed ability groupings.* Maidenhead: Open University Press.

Goodyear, V.A. & Casey, A. (2015). Innovation with change: Developing a community of practice to help teachers move beyond the 'honeymoon' of pedagogical renovation. *Physical Education and Sport Pedagogy, 20*(2), 186–203.

Kelly, M.P., & Barker, M. (2016). Why is changing health-related behaviour so difficult? *Public Health, 136,* 109–116.

Kemmis, S. (2009). Action research as a practice-based practice, *Educational Action Research, 17*(3), 463–474.

Kemmis, S., & Grootenboer, P. (2008). Situating praxis in practice: Practice architectures and the cultural, social and material conditions for practice. In S. Kemmis and T.J. Smith (eds), *Enabling praxis: challenges for education* (pp. 37–62). Rotterdam: Sense Publishers.

Larsson, H., & Redelius, K. (2004) *Mellan nytta och nöje: Bilder av ämnet idrott och.* Stockholm: Idrottshögskola.

Lawson, H.A. (1993). Teachers' uses of research in practice: A literature review. *Journal of Teaching in Physical Education, 12*(4), 366–374.

McCambridge, J., Witton, J., & Elbourne, D.R. (2014). Systematic review of the Hawthorne effect: New concepts are needed to study research participation effects. *Journal of Clinical Epidemiology, 67*(3), 267–277.

Schön, D.A. (1983). *The reflective practitioner: How professionals think in action.* New York: Basic Books.

Sparkes, A.C. (1988). The micropolitics of innovation in the physical education curriculum. In J. Evans (Ed.), *Teachers, teaching and control in physical education* (pp. 157–177). Lewes: Falmer Press.

Stenhouse, L. (1981). What counts as research? *British Journal of Educational Studies, 29*(2), 102–114.

Tinning, R. (2014). Reading self-study in/for physical education: Revisiting the zeitgeist of reflection. In A. Ovens & T. Fletcher (eds), *Self-study in physical education teacher education* (pp. 153–167). Dordrecht: Springer.

Williams, R. (1977). *Marxism and literature.* London: Oxford University Press.

PART II

The four chapters that make up Part II each focus on one of the methodologies we have chosen to help practitioners conduct research. The methodologies are presented chronologically as our intent has been to follow, fairly closely, the order in which they appeared in the discourse of educational research. Thus, we begin with action research (first appearing in about 1946), followed by narrative inquiry (throughout the 1980s), autoethnography (throughout the 1990s), and self-study of practice (throughout the late 1990s and 2000s).

In each chapter we trace the history of the methodology back to its inception and examine early, seminal texts. Following a brief overview of the early history of the methodology we discuss the key features of each approach and provide examples of how practitioners have already begun to use these approaches in the study of personal pedagogy. Each chapter also includes a section about how the methodology has been used by practitioner researchers in physical education and youth sport.

Although all four of us contributed to the chapters in some way, we each took the lead on one of the chapters based on our experience with, and knowledge of, the different methodologies. Given his record of publishing action research studies, Ash led the action research chapter. Following the same rationale, Lee led the chapter on narrative inquiry, Doug the autoethnography chapter and Tim the self-study of practice chapter. The reason we explain this now is because readers will likely notice some differences and idiosyncrasies in the writing style in each chapter. We make no apologies for this as we did not want to feel trapped by conforming to one particular style. Indeed, the style of writing is something that is vitally important in reading exemplars from the four methodologies, as is giving agency and voice to the practitioner researcher.

2

ACTION RESEARCH

What is action research?

As an educator or coach, you may already be aware of, if not familiar, with action research. However, it may be helpful to define what it is and what it isn't. In their point-by-point guide Henry and Kemmis (1985, p. 1) defined action research as:

> a form of self-reflective enquiry undertaken by participants in social situations in order to improve the rationality and justice in their own social or educational practices, as well as their own understanding of these practices and the situations in which these practices are carried out.

Put succinctly, Henry and Kemmis (1985) argue that action research is undertaken by a person (or persons) in their own context to improve their practice, their understanding of their practice and their understanding of the location in which they practice. They further suggested that action research is: (a) not the usual thing teachers do when they think about their teaching, (b) not problem-solving as much as it was problem-posing, (c) not research on other people and it does not treat others as objects, instead it is about helping people improve what they do, and (d) not a scientific method applied to teaching (in other words, it is not about hypothesis-testing).

At its heart, action research is about improving by learning and changing from within. It often starts small, is participatory, collaborative and inclusive. It utilises a self-reflective spiral and it encourages an open-minded, systematic, developmental approach. Ultimately, action researchers focus on developing, testing and critically examining the actions they take in their own pedagogical spaces. In short, action research is an approach used to shed light on a situation and change it. Certainly, the intention is that such change is for the better but that may not always be the case. Sometimes a practitioner is influenced by the ideas of another – by a book or an observation – but when they try it in their own context it doesn't work as hoped. This is not a bad thing and if action research (or any of the approaches in this book) can help you to see and understand your own context better, we see this as successful research.

A number of researchers have written about and developed detailed and expressive explanations of the action research methodology. At the heart of these 'definitions' are five cornerstones (adapted from Altrichter, Posch, & Somekh, 1993; Carr & Kemmis, 1986; Elliott, 1991; Ponte, 2002; Stenhouse, 1981):

(1) *The practitioner* – who is both central to and active in the process of actioning research.
(2) *Self-reflection* – which is used to allow the practitioner to plan, act, observe, and build more refined plans for action.
(3) *The social situation* – which is the context in which the study occurs. This is not neutral space but is one where relationships, expectations and practices butt against each other and influence what can and cannot be done.
(4) *Improving practice* – which, we argue, should be at the heart of every practitioner's journey. It is not enough to simply stand still. And . . .
(5) *Ethics* – Teaching and coaching are ethical practices. It is a practitioner's responsibility to teach to the very best of his or her ability. It is a practitioner's responsibility to put the needs of his or her charges first. And it is a practitioner's responsibility to ensure that what they are moving towards is better than what they are leaving behind.

These cornerstones stand as the fundamental tenets to action research. Each can be seen as a construct that guides your choice and use of action research. If you can use these as filters through which to improve your practice then you will, we believe, be moving towards change.

What are the main features of action research?

It is important to acknowledge that action research is not 'one thing' but is 'best thought of as a large family, one in which beliefs and relationships vary greatly' (Noffke, 1997, p. 306). It is not a discrete way of doing research as much as it is a conglomeration of ideas that have emerged over time and across different contexts.

The resurgence of action research from its roots in the 1940s, especially in education, is credited to the work of Lawrence Stenhouse and his efforts to emphasise:

> the process of making public the systematic inquires of teachers in order to affect other teachers, but also the larger educational community (Stenhouse, 1983). [Stenhouse's work] represents the beginnings of contemporary

attempts to place the work of teachers within a larger sphere of questions of knowledge claims, or epistemology, in educational research.

(Noffke, 1997, p. 323)

Stenhouse had a significant impact on both educational action research in a general sense and our interpretation of action research for this chapter/book. Fundamentally, like Stenhouse, we endorse the central role that participants play in pedagogical and curriculum development (in his case it was teachers but we feel it could equally be coaches). Like Stenhouse (1975) and others after him (see Saunders & Somekh, 2009), we believe that positive social change doesn't occur under its own steam or simply because someone asked for it. Instead, it takes ongoing interactions between pedagogues, learners and context.

In his seminal paper 'Action research and minority problems', Lewin (1946) carefully laid out his vision for the cyclical process of 'actioned' research which involved five sequential objectives (Figure 2.1). In this model, the practitioner is encouraged to undertake a series of cycles that focus on five concepts (Table 2.1).

As the practitioner moves into subsequent cycles of action research, he or she moves from the reflection stage back to thinking (6) (now labelled re-think) which allows for the creation of new plans (7), fresh actions (8), new evaluations (9) and further reflections (10) in an ongoing cycle with the ultimate aim of improving practice.

Lewin (1946, p. 38) summarised action research as 'a spiral of steps each of which is composed of a circle of planning, action and fact-finding about the result of the action'. However, we argue that these steps are taken on numerous levels; not exclusively including the micro steps taken on a daily, lesson-by-lesson basis and the macro steps taken across the life of the study. Figure 2.2 is included as a means of conceptualising the multiplicity and differing longevity of the various cycles within cycles within an action research project.

In presenting this conceptualisation of action research we contest the limited notion of the complete action research cycle offered by Meyer, Hamilton, Kroeger, and Stewart (2004) as being from the initial conceptualisation of a research question to the publication of research paper. The range and assortment of complete 'experimental cycles of action' (Elliott & Tsai, 2008, p. 575)

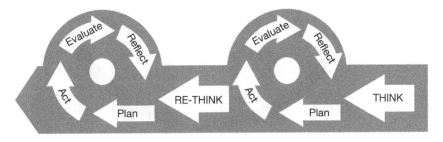

FIGURE 2.1 The cyclical process of action research.

TABLE 2.1 The five stages of action research.

1. Think	In Lewin's initial conception of action research, the starting point is the identification of a general problem or idea. For teachers and coaches, the idea may emerge from a game, a lesson or a practice, a parent meeting, or a student/player observation. It might be a decision to use a different pedagogical approach, be more learner-centred or have a focus on game tactics rather than learning skills and techniques.
2. Plan	Next, the practitioner engages in a period of planning and settles on an initial way to approach the idea or problem. In this way the practitioner plans before acting. Pedagogical change, through action research, is not undertaken on a whim but is something that is planned for.
3. Act	The third of Lewin's steps is action itself. Having developed a plan, a practitioner would put it into play in the first lesson/session and attempt to address the problem or idea through his or her practice.
4. Evaluate	Following this initial action, the practitioner engages in evaluation (e.g. observation, data gathering) in order to begin to understand how actioning the plan impacted on learning and, consequently, how it might have affected his or her initial thinking.
5. Reflect	The information gained from the evaluation step allows the action researcher to reflect on the action taken and the learning it engendered. Such fact-finding allows the practitioner to be scrutinised in an effort to gauge the strengths and weaknesses of their plan, facilitate improvements in planning, and allow for modifications in the overall plan (if needed).

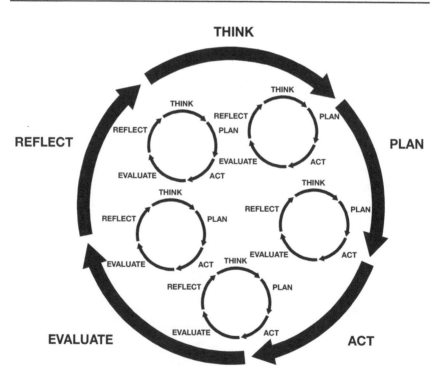

FIGURE 2.2 A conceptualisation of the multiplicity and longevity of action research as cycles within cycles.

contained within action research is such that multiple cycles are undertaken in any one study; each with its own beginning and end. Consequently, each cycle is unrestrained by depth or time and therefore the lifetime of action research should be viewed in multiple cycles, not as a stand-alone event; in other words, as cycles within cycles (Casey, 2010).

A brief history of action research

Action research emerged from the field of social psychology in the 1940s as a means of 'promoting positive social change' (Lewin, 1946, p. 390) and as a form of 'action-research, research-action' (Collier, 1945). More recently, action research has been lauded because 'it makes a direct contribution to transformative action and to *changing history* . . . the first concern of action researchers should be *the contribution of their action to history, not so much to theory*' (Kemmis, 2010, p. 425; original emphasis).

The two men credited with the development of action research, John Collier and Kurt Lewin, both published their works within months of each other. However, while it is Lewin's work that has been internationally acclaimed (see Noffke, 1997) the contribution of John Collier should not be overlooked. In his earliest work, Collier (1945) highlighted the need for knowledge to be fed directly into action. It is important to note that the knowledge he identified was not simply the academically approved works of research but the layperson's lived understandings and experiences. His foregrounding of *in situ* knowledge is fundamentally important to action research as it prioritises the knowledge and expertise of laypeople such as teachers and coaches. Collier's drive was to ensure that both time and opportunity for change were afforded to those who knew the situation best.

In the early 1950s, Stephen Corey and a larger group of educational researchers at Columbia University brought action research into education. Noffke (1997, p. 316) suggested that Corey and colleagues 'were supportive of classroom teachers' knowledge' while remaining sceptical of educational research. By the end of the 1950s, action research had become more about personal and professional learning and was increasingly focused on the individual teacher. While action research went 'out of vogue' in the 1960s, it enjoyed a resurgence in the 1970s in the UK as a result of the work of Lawrence Stenhouse (Noffke, 1997).

At the heart of action research is a curiosity and a desire to understand that is systematic (inasmuch as it is rigorous) and public (inasmuch as it should be open to critical public scrutiny). As Stenhouse (1983, p. 178) argued:

> To call for research-based teaching is, I suggest, to ask us as teachers to share with our pupils or students the process of our learning the wisdom which we do not possess so that they can get into critical perspective the learning which we trust is ours.

Put differently, Stenhouse (1979) felt that by presenting ourselves as foolproof and our knowledge as watertight we give those under our charge a false impression of learning. In other words, as a fixed entity. He argued that under the guise of infallibility, we present learning as a process driven by conclusions and end points rather than as a voyage of discovery. In contrast, Stenhouse felt that research-based practice should be used to help learners to understand that doubt, bewilderment, obscurity and contradiction are at the heart of teaching and learning.

Doing action research

The key in action research is that the work is carried out by someone personally concerned with the social situation. It begins with questions about practice in everyday pedagogical situations, uses simple methods and is 'defined by continuing effort to closely interlink, relate and confront action and reflection' (Altrichter et al., 1993, p. 6). In what remains of this chapter, we explore action research through a series of characteristics: who (in the field, by the field), what (emergent processes that embody values, philosophy in action and change) and why (outcomes and, rationale) before talking about action research in physical education and youth sport.

Who? (In the field, by the field)

Action research is conducted in the field by someone native to the field (Noffke & Zeichner, 1987). Action research isn't about proving that something we already know and do is right. Instead it is about aiding the action taker to do his or her job better, rather than simply the same. In contrast to traditional educational research, which Corey defined as fundamental research aimed at establishing 'new generalisations stated as observed uniformities, explanatory principles, or scientific laws' (Corey, 1949, p. 257), action research is about studying certain learners, in certain spaces, in a certain school or club, in a certain city, and improving their education.

Drawing on the work of Noffke (1997) and Noffke and Zeichner (1987), Zeichner (2003) outlined three underlying motivations behind a practitioner's research into their own practices: (1) to better understand and improve their own practices; (2) to produce knowledge for others to use; and (3) to address issues of social inequality and enhance democracy.

What? (An emergent process that embodies values, philosophy in action and change)

It has been argued that in the very act of problematising and improving teaching/coaching, our underlying philosophies and ideologies about teaching/coaching become our practices; that is, our 'way of life' (Kemmis, 2010, p. 418) and our 'ways of being' (Feldman & Weiss, 2010, p. 30). Action research, in this way, is an emergent process with the 'core principle [of combining] action with research [and] challenging the routines of the status quo' (Somekh & Zeichner, 2009, p. 19).

In his early work, Elliott (1976) held that in the very process of challenging commonly held expectations about teaching and teachers (we add coaching and coaches), the potential emerged to develop a profession that was self-monitoring. In other words, action research provides a place where practitioners have established the long-term habits of reflection and self-evaluation (Noffke & Zeichner, 1987). Such notions of quality assurance position action research as an undertaking that leads practitioners to enhance their normal practices and then, in turn, to make these enhanced practices the norm. This then requires more action research to enhance and change these new norms, and so on and so forth *ad infinitum*.

These 'enhanced normal practices' (Feldman, 1996, p. 27) – in fact the whole-sale changes to a practitioner's 'attitudes, beliefs and stances' (Feldman & Weiss, 2010, p. 32) – are often seen as the goal of action research. Consequently, action research is not something that is done to practitioners but instead it becomes something that is embedded in daily practices (Goodnough, 2010). In this way, the fundamental precept of action research becomes the study of things by chang-ing them within their natural habitat (Adelman, 1993). In other words, action research is practically embedded in the practice context (Ax, Ponte & Brouwer, 2008) and adheres to the notion that teachers and coaches can understand and change their own lives by mixing research, education and action (Brydon-Miller & Maguire, 2009).

Why? Outcomes and rationale

Much has been written about action research and the outcomes it seeks to attain. In his review of research related to the professional development impact of school-based teacher research programmes in the USA, Zeichner suggested that teacher research 'has often had a profound effect on those who have done it, in some cases transforming the classrooms and schools in which they work' (Zeichner, 2003, p. 303). In this review Zeichner identified eight self-reported outcomes that had emerged from research over the previous two decades. Sixteen years earlier Noffke and Zeichner (1987, pp. 4–5) had also developed a series of eight categories that, in their words, 'clarify and describe those qualities of thought that could be, or are believed to be, affected by action research' (see Table 2.2). While we acknowledge that these reviews were undertaken on teachers and teaching, we hold that their findings are equally relevant to coaches and coaching.

These findings support much of what has been written about action research in terms of changing practices and engendering discernible improvements at the class-room/group and school/club level. However, these outcomes do not occur either easily or automatically. If they did then perhaps action research would be the pro-fessional development strategy of choice in every school, sports club and country. This isn't the case and there needs to be a reason for teachers and coaches to engage in this type of research in the first place and then to sustain it over several weeks, months or (possibly) years. If the aim is to improve practice and have practitio-ners who are self-reflective in their social situation, focused on improving practice

TABLE 2.2 A comparison of the outcomes of action research.

Noffke and Zeichner (1987)	Zeichner (2003)	Overarching themes
Changes how teacher defines professional skills and roles		Changing teacher 'skill set' and role
Broader view of teaching, schooling and society		Enhanced conception of education
	More proactive and self-directed in relation to external authority	Increased autonomy
Increased self-worth and confidence	Enhance self-esteem and confidence	Enhanced self-esteem/confidence
Increased confluence between teachers' theories and practices Increase in teachers' awareness of/changes in specific beliefs	Narrowing of the gap between aspiration and practice Increased teacher flexibility and openness to new ideas	Classroom practice better reflects teacher beliefs
Enhanced disposition towards reflection	Development of self-analysis skills which can be applied elsewhere	'Self-aware teachers'
	Changing communication between teachers and enhanced collegiality	Teaching as a public act
Changes in teachers' development stages		Increased maturation of teachers
Increases teachers' awareness of classroom events	Conversations move away from student problems and towards accomplishment Greater awareness of student achievement	Aware of the classroom around their practices

and acting ethically, then action research may be the means through which such change is made.

How action research has been used in physical education and youth sport

Despite the attention action research has been given by some academics in physical education (Kirk, 1986; Tinning, 1992) it is reputed to have made little impact in the field of research on teaching in physical education. Rossi and Tan (2012) argued that there had been relatively little action research undertaken in physical education and youth sport. While we have no reason to doubt Rossi and Tan, we feel that action research has had a bigger effect. That said, we also feel that much of what was presented as action research isn't action research; at least not as we recognise it.

Therefore, and in seeking to support or refute Rossi and Tan's claim (ibid.), we undertook a review of the action research literature in sport, physical education and coaching. In doing so, our aim was to: (a) disrupt the idea that there was very little action research undertaken in either physical education or youth sport, and (b) highlight different ways in which action research has been used effectively in our field.

Our search revealed 100+ papers professing to use action research in physical education and youth sport. Of these we were able to access 55 papers for further exploration. University journal subscriptions (or a lack of them), language (a number were written in languages other than English – predominantly Spanish and Portuguese) and format (i.e. conference abstracts) were the predominant reasons that papers were excluded from our review.

We termed the largest category of studies (with 36 papers) as superficial. This represents a significant body of research in which authors stated that action research was used but provided little further information. Ten papers were categorised as good because they both explored the action research literature and demonstrated how the methodology informed the analysis and results (see Casey, 2013a; Casey, Dyson & Campbell, 2009; Cassady, Clarke & Latham, 2004; Enright & O'Sullivan, 2010, 2012; Enright, Coll, Ní Chróinín & Fitzpatrick, 2016; Garrett & Wrench, 2016a, 2016b; Goodyear & Casey, 2015; Hall & Gray, 2016). We categorised nine papers as exemplars (see Bodsworth & Goodyear, 2017; Casey & Dyson, 2009; Casey, 2012; Farias, Hastie & Mesquita, 2017; Glotova & Hastie, 2014; Hopper, 1997; Keegan, 2016; Robinson, Walters & Francis, 2016; Sum et al., 2016). What these papers have in common is the explicit way action research is positioned as central to the study. It is not something that is talked about but is something that is actioned and researched. In the table below, we have shared what some of these exemplar studies looked at and how action research helped the researchers rethink their practice.

TABLE 2.3 Changes made as a result of action research (excluding Ash's work).

Paper	Topic	Changes made because of action research
Hopper (1997)	Action research was used to develop relationships between supervising and student-teachers. The overarching aim was to empower student-teachers to self-direct their own development as teachers.	Hooper, in conjunction with his teacher education students and school-based supervising teachers, used action research to free trainee teachers from the didactic pedagogies of their past. By engaging all parties in the action research process, trainees and supervising teachers alike were more prepared to use innovative pedagogies learnt in university.

(*Continued*)

TABLE 2.3 (*Continued*)

Paper	Topic	Changes made because of action research
Glotova and Hastie (2014)	This study of student teachers' introduction to the sport education model used action research to explore: (1) How well the students understood the principles and philosophies of sport education? (2) To what extent students intend to implement Sport Education in their future teaching?	The steps inherent in action research helped the researchers to reflect on what they saw, heard and noted during the intervention. Action research helped both teachers new to sport education and the researcher to keep motivation and interest levels high as they negotiated the use of a new pedagogical model.
Keegan (2016)	Action research itself was under scrutiny in this study. The researcher employed it to assess its effectiveness as an agent of change and its impact on enhancing her teaching and the learning experience of her students in physical education.	Whilst action research was used throughout the paper to frame the author's argument, it was used particularly effectively to both articulate the issues she identified and the manner and week this issue was addressed. Furthermore, Keegan used action research to map the effects of her interventions on both herself (as the teacher) and her pupils.
Robinson, Walters and Francis (2016)	Having identified limitations in student-teacher practicum/ school experience, the authors used action research to pilot, shape and negotiate a new form of practicum that sought to enhance mentor-protégé relationships.	Action research was used in this teacher education programme to take risks and test potential alternative approaches. Indeed, the authors termed their use of action research as a 'pilot inquiry approach' (PIA) and stated their intention to use PIA as a 'way of visioning future responsive teacher education programs' (p. 53).
Sum et al. (2016)	In their exploration of how practitioners at multiple levels of education progress in physical education these researchers used action research as a means of moving belief about physical education to the culture of physical education.	In this study action research was used mainly as a means of scaffolding and making explicit the reflections of the teachers. The structure offered by action research helped teachers realise how 'their teaching styles may have been personalized according to their intentions and beliefs' (p. 14).

Paper	Topic	Changes made because of action research
Farias et al. (2017)	Action research was used across four consecutive seasons of sport education to help the authors explore (a) the ways in which a teacher supported three student-coaches develop their instructional leadership, and (b) the manner in which the self-same coaches involved their peers in their own learning.	In reporting on four separate cycles of action research the authors were able to highlight a number of key findings. First, they identified a need to support higher order learning when teacher modelling. Second, the researchers explored the manner in which interactions were structured between student-coaches and their peers. Third, researchers used action research to better understand ways of handing over increased responsibility to student-coaches for skill development. Finally, action research was used to introduce and scaffold peer teaching activities.
Bodsworth and Goodyear (2017)	The authors used action research to focus on a teacher-researcher's use of iPads within a cooperative learning track and field unit. The methodology was used as professional development to refine the teacher-researcher's practice.	The authors argue that action research served as a key facilitator in learning how to use digital technology to support learning. Indeed, they held that action research could be 'used as a key driver to support teachers learning how to incorporate digital technologies into their classrooms' (p. 15).

When action research is undertaken in this way it gives us (as individuals and as a community) a 'fly on the wall' look into the impact of research conducted in the field by someone native to the field (Noffke & Zeichner, 1987). In many ways, 'unless we acknowledge that pedagogical change takes time and is achieved over a number of individual steps, rather than simply being a journey to celebrate, then we will continue to have an 'airbrushed' view of the destination, rather than understanding that difficult steps were required to reach it' (Casey, 2013b, p. 161). Teaching and coaching are complex processes. We shouldn't Photoshop out the rigours, trials and tribulations of change. It is important to acknowledge the hard parts. But nor should we hide our successes. Action research is a way of seeing both challenges and successes through a cycle of change. The key, and what the nine papers we have highlighted as exemplars succeed in doing, is showing how this occurs and why.

Further reading/key texts/annotated bibliography

Based on our researching of key papers in action research in physical education and youth sport above, we recommend each of the nine papers to the reader as examples of how action research, when done well, is central to pedagogical change.

The possibilities of action research in physical education and youth sport

By understanding that steps and not just journeys are important we begin to see how change occurs. In the cycles of think, plan, act, evaluate, reflect, *the practitioner*, through *self-reflection*, seeks to better understand *the social situation* in which the study occurs and improve future *practice*. It is an *ethical* process in which change is built on both present day understanding and future improvements. The different cycles of action research are aimed at helping practitioners to enhance their normal practices and then make these enhanced practices the norm. With the criticisms that are regularly levelled at physical education and youth sport it seems that action research presents us with a prime opportunity to enhance our practice.

References

Adelman, C. (1993). Kurt Lewin and the origins of action research. *Educational Action Research, 1*(1), 7–24.

Altrichter, H., Posch, P., & Somekh, B. (1993). *Teachers investigate their work: An introduction to the methods of action research*. London: Routledge.

Ax, J., Ponte, P., & Brouwer, N. (2008). Action research in initial teacher education: an explorative study. *Educational Action Research, 16*(1), 55–72.

Bodsworth, H., & Goodyear, V. A. (2017). Barriers and facilitators to using digital technologies in the Cooperative Learning model in physical education, *Physical Education and Sport Pedagogy*, iFirst, doi.org/10.1080/17408989.2017.1294672

Brydon-Miller, M., & Maguire, P. (2009). Participatory action research: Contributions to the development of practitioner inquiry in education. *Educational Action Research, 17*(1), 79–93.

Carr, W., & Kemmis, S. (1986). *Becoming critical: Education, knowledge, and action research*. London: Falmer Press.

Casey, A. (2010). Practitioner research in physical education: Teacher transformation through pedagogical and curricular change. Unpublished doctoral dissertation, Leeds Metropolitan University.

Casey, A. (2012). A self-study using action research: Changing site expectations and practice stereotypes. *Educational Action Research, 20*(2), 219–232.

Casey, A. (2013a). Practitioner research: A means of coping with the systemic demands for continual professional development? *European Physical Education Review, 19*(1), 70–84.

Casey, A. (2013b). 'Seeing the trees not just the wood': Steps and not just journeys in teacher action research. *Educational Action Research, 21*(2), 147–163.

Casey, A., & Dyson, B. (2009). The implementation of models-based practice in physical education through action research. *European Physical Education Review, 15*(2), 175–199.

Casey, A., Dyson, B., & Campbell, A. (2009). Action research in physical education: Focusing beyond myself through cooperative learning. *Educational Action Research, 17*(3), 407–423.

Cassady, H., Clarke, G., & Latham, A.-M. (2004). Experiencing evaluation: A case study of girls' dance. *Physical Education & Sport Pedagogy*, *9*(1), 22–36.

Collier, J. (1945). United States Indian Administration as a laboratory of ethnic relations. *Social Research*, *12*(3), 265–303.

Corey, S.M. (1949). Curriculum development through action research. *Educational Leadership*, *7*, 147–153.

Elliott, J. (1976). Preparing teachers for classroom accountability. *Education for Teaching*, *100*, 49–71.

Elliott, J. (1991). A model of professionalism and its implications for teacher education. *British Educational Research Journal*, *17*(4), 309–318.

Elliott, J., & Tsai, C. (2008). What might Confucius have to say about action research? *Educational Action Research*, *16*(4), 569–578.

Enright, E., Coll, L., Ní Chróinín, D., & Fitzpatrick, M. (2016). Student voice as risky praxis: Democratising physical education teacher education. *Physical Education and Sport Pedagogy*, iFirst: doi.org/10.1080/17408989.2016.1225031.

Enright, E., & O'Sullivan, M. (2010). 'Can I do it in my pyjamas?' Negotiating a physical education curriculum with teenage girls. *European Physical Education Review*, *16*(3), 203–222.

Enright, E., & O'Sullivan, M. (2012). Physical education 'in all sorts of corners': Student activists transgressing formal physical education curricular boundaries. *Research Quarterly for Exercise and Sport*, *83*(2), 255–267.

Farias, C., Hastie, P.A., & Mesquita, I. (2017). Scaffolding student-coaches' instructional leadership toward student-centred peer interactions: A yearlong action-research intervention in Sport Education. *European Physical Education Review*, online early. doi. org/10.1177/1356336X16687303.

Feldman, A. (1996). Enhancing the practice of physics teachers: Mechanisms for the generation and sharing of knowledge and understanding in collaborative action research. *Journal of Research in Science Teaching*, *33*, 513–540.

Feldman, A., & Weiss, T. (2010). Understanding change in teachers' ways of being through collaborative action research: A cultural–historical activity theory analysis. *Educational Action Research*, *18*(1), 29–55.

Garrett, R., & Wrench, A. (2016a). 'If they can say it they can write it': Inclusive pedagogies for senior secondary physical education. *International Journal of Inclusive Education*, *20*(5), 486–502.

Garrett, R., & Wrench, A. (2016b). Redesigning pedagogy for boys and dance in physical education. *European Physical Education Review*, doi.org/10.1177/1356336X16668201.

Glotova, O.N., & Hastie, P.A. (2014). Learning to teach Sport Education in Russia: Factors affecting model understanding and intentions to teach. *Sport Education and Society*, *19*(8), 1072–1088.

Goodnough, K. (2010). The role of action research in transforming teacher identity: Modes of belonging and ecological perspectives. *Educational Action Research*, *18*(2), 167–182.

Goodyear, V.A., & Casey, A. (2015). Innovation with change: Developing a community of practice to help teachers move beyond the 'honeymoon' of pedagogical renovation. *Physical Education and Sport Pedagogy*, *20*(2), 186–203.

Hall, E.T., & Gray, S. (2016). Reflecting on reflective practice: A coach's action research narratives. *Qualitative Research in Sport, Exercise and Health*, *8*(4), 365–379.

Henry, C., & Kemmis, S. (1985). A point-by-point guide to action research for teachers. *The Australian Administrator*, *6*(6), 65–72.

Hopper, T.F. (1997). Learning to respond: Supervising novice physical educators in an action research project. *Sport, Education & Society*, *2*(2), 163–180.

Keegan, R. (2016). Action research as an agent for enhancing teaching and learning in physical education: A physical education teacher's perspective. *The Physical Educator, 73*, 255–284.

Kemmis, S. (2010). What is to be done? The place of action research. *Educational Action Research, 18*(4), 417–427.

Kirk, D. (1986). A critical pedagogy for teacher education: Toward an inquiry-oriented approach. *Journal of Teaching in Physical Education, 5*(4), 230–246.

Lewin, K. (1946). Action research and minority problems. *Journal of Social Issues, 2*(4), 34–46.

Meyer, H., Hamilton, B., Kroeger, S., & Stewart, S. (2004). The unexpected journey: Renewing our commitment to students through educational action research. *Educational Action Research, 12*(4), 557–574.

Noffke, S. (1997). Themes and tensions in US action research: Towards historical analysis. In S. Hollingsworth (ed.), *International action research: A casebook for* (pp. 2–16). London: Routledge.

Noffke, S., & Zeichner, K. (1987). Action research and teacher thinking: The first phase of the action research on action research project at the University of Wisconsin-Madison. Paper Presented at Annual Meeting of the American Educational Research Association.

Ponte, P. (2002). How teachers become action researchers and how teacher educators become their facilitators. *Educational Action Research, 10*(3), 399–422.

Robinson, D. B., Walters, W., & Francis, S. (2016). Exploring other practicum possibilities: An action research initiative. *Canadian Journal of Action Research, 17*(3), 39–56.

Rossi, A., & Tan, W. K. (2012). Action research in physical education: Cyclers, not circles! In K. M. Armour & D. Macdonald (eds), *Research Methods in Physical Education and Youth Sport* (pp. 250–262). London: Routledge.

Saunders, L., & Somekh, B. (2009). Action research and educational change: the professional voice of teachers in curriculum and pedagogy. In S. Noffke & B. Somekh (eds), *Handbook of Educational Action Research* (pp. 190–201). London: Sage Publications.

Somekh, B., & Zeichner, K. (2009). Action research for educational reform: Remodelling action research theories and practices in local contexts. *Educational Action Research, 17*(1), 5–21.

Stenhouse, L. (1975). *An introduction to curriculum research and development*. London: Heinemann.

Stenhouse, L. (1979). Research as the basis for teaching. Inaugural lecture at the University of East Anglia, Norwich, England, 20 February. Subsequently published in L. Stenhouse, *Authority, Education and Emancipation* (London: Heinemann Educational, 1983).

Stenhouse, L. (1981). What counts as research? *British Journal of Educational Studies, 29*(2), 103–114.

Stenhouse, L. (1983). The relevance of practice to theory. *Theory into Practice, 22*(3), 211–215.

Sum, R. K. W., Ma, M. S., Ha, A. S., Tang, T. M., Shek, C. K., Cheng, C. L., & Kong, F. (2016). Action research exploring Chinese physical education teachers' value of physical education: From belief to culture. *Asia Pacific Journal of Sport and Social Science, 5*(1), 70–84.

Tinning, R. (1992). Reading action research – notes on knowledge and human interests. *Quest, 44*(1), 1–14.

Zeichner, K. M. (2003). Teacher research as professional development P-12 educators in the USA. *Educational Action Research, 11*(2), 301–326.

3

NARRATIVE INQUIRY

Introduction

It was my first master's class. I had never really identified myself as a student, so starting a master's came with much trepidation. But, as a third year physical education teacher, I had so many questions that I needed answers to, in particular, why teachers', particularly physical educators, knowledge seemed to be marginalised on a daily basis. The first half of the course was difficult. I felt like each of the articles I read wrote over the teachers and the students. I was convinced that if this is what the researchers were interested in, that this route was not going to be for me. About halfway through semester, I remember putting off my readings all week, and it was now the evening before our master's course. I was exhausted from a full day of teaching but willed myself to at least read a few pages before falling asleep. The article 'Stories of experience and narrative inquiry' caught my attention immediately as it discussed the importance of teachers' experiences, how much we can learn from teachers, and how important their knowledge is in re-defining education. I remember thinking that perhaps educational research was for me if I could do it this way.

(Lee Schaefer, journal entry from a Master's course, 2008)

This chapter is not about narrative research in general but more specifically about Clandinin and Connelly's conception of narrative inquiry (Connelly & Clandinin, 1990; Clandinin & Connelly 2000; Clandinin, 2013). There is much confusion in the education literature around narrative research and narrative inquiry, which makes it difficult for those new to the methodology to specifically understand how to use narrative inquiry as a research method. In this chapter I attempt to clearly outline the main features of narrative inquiry from Connelly and Clandanin's conception (1990).

Distinguishing between narrative research and narrative inquiry

'What narrative researchers hold in common is the study of stories or narratives or descriptions of a series of events' (Pinnegar & Daynes, 2007, p. 5). Narrative research thus refers to research conducted by those individuals who use narrative methodologies and utilise participants' stories as data. The commonalities end there as narrative researchers take up diverse approaches, study designs, methodologies, analyses and forms of representation. Clandinin (2013) suggests that while many narrative methodologies are used to think *about* stories, narrative inquiry (Clandinin and Connelly, 2000) is used to think *with* stories. If this still seems confusing, you are not alone as defining narrative inquiry is a complex task. However, there is some agreement on the following definition:

> People shape their daily lives by stories of who they and others are and as they interpret their past in terms of these stories. Story, in the current idiom, is a portal through which a person enters the world and by which their experience of the world is interpreted and made personally meaningful. Narrative inquiry, the study of experience as story, then, is first and foremost a way of thinking about experience. Narrative inquiry as a methodology entails a view of the phenomenon. To use narrative inquiry methodology is to adopt a particular view of experience as phenomenon under study.
>
> *(Connelly & Clandinin, 2006, p. 375)*

We see in this definition that narrative inquiry is both a methodology as well as the phenomenon under study. So, while you are using the methodology of narrative inquiry, the phenomenon under study is also narratives and how they allow us to better understand experience. We also see that narrative inquiry includes a particular way of thinking about experience. This will become clearer in the detailed outline of the main features of narrative inquiry.

Narrative inquirers are specifically concerned with individuals' lived experiences within the world. As Clandinin and Connelly (2000, p. 20) state:

> Narrative inquiry is a way of understanding experience. It is collaboration between researcher and participants, over time, in a place or series of places, and in social interaction with milieus. An inquirer enters this matrix in the midst and progresses in the same spirit, concluding the inquiry still in the midst of living and telling, reliving and retelling, the stories of the experiences that made up people's lives, both individual and social.

Important to note here is that unlike some other narrative research methodologies, narrative inquiry cannot be boiled down to stories. This is a common misconception held by many graduate students and researchers. I often hear those interested in narrative inquiry advocating for the importance of stories and, in particular, how important it is to listen to others' stories. While hearing others' stories is important, it becomes easy to see how, from an empirical research perspective (that is, research published in academic journals), critiques about rigour and lack of theoretical underpinnings can stem from this confusion and, in turn, create false assumptions about what narrative inquiry is.

Paying careful attention to the quotation by Clandinin and Connelly (2000), we see that narrative inquiry is a way of understanding experience in relationship to the researchers' experiences, the participants' experiences, both bound in time, the social environment and place. It is in trying to understand others' experiences that story becomes important, as it affords us a portal, a window, into how individuals understand their own experiences, how we may understand these experiences as researchers and, in turn, how these experiences make up people's lives.

In the opening story fragment, I used one of my own experiences to give a sense of how I was drawn to narrative inquiry. While my initial understandings of narrative inquiry may not have been accurate, there was something that resonated with me in regard to actually paying attention to what research participants were saying as being important; paying attention to their knowledge. As I experienced reading other educational research, I felt that teachers' and students' experiences were explained away by theories, models and frameworks that in many ways over-wrote who they were. In my opinion, educational research did not provide an authentic representation of teachers' and students' voices. I did not feel this way as I read my first narrative inquiry article. My reading of narrative inquiry made me feel as though teachers' knowledge mattered and, in a roundabout way, this meant that my knowledge mattered. In looking at the initial beginnings of the narrative inquiry movement, one might say that it was seeing teachers as knowl-edge holders that provided the impetus for narrative inquiry as a methodology (Clandinin, Schaefer, & Downey, 2014). When working with graduate students, this is one of the aspects of narrative inquiry that resonates with those interested in narrative inquiry. In this way, narrative inquiry represents a particular view of the world that values and upholds the knowledge that participants bring to the research endeavour.

What are the main features of narrative inquiry?

While there are a number of features that distinguish narrative inquiry from other narrative research methods and other research methods – like action research or ethnography (Clandinin & Rosiek, 2007; Pinnegar & Daynes, 2007) – in this sec-tion I will focus on the philosophical underpinnings of narrative inquiry as well as the metaphorical 'three dimensional narrative inquiry space'.

Our attempt in this book is to help both teachers and researchers take up these methodologies. Given that I see teachers as knowledge holders, I won't apologise for delving into the philosophical underpinnings of narrative inquiry. I don't do this to give the chapter rigour (although it may from a theoretical perspective). I do this because it helps those new to the methodology to understand why narrative inquiry might be seen as distinct from other narrative research method-ologies and in a broader sense why narrative inquirers value experience, people's knowledge and people's lives.

Ontological commitment

Narrative inquiry begins with an ontological commitment to experience. Plainly stated, ontology is the study of reality; how phenomena become real. The ontolog-ical commitment of narrative inquiry stems from John Dewey's (1938) pragmatic ontology that characterises reality as living within an individual's experiences. In other words, what you see (and hear, feel, think, love, taste, despise, fear, etc.) is what you get. That is all we ultimately have in which to ground our understand-ing. And that is all we need (Clandinin & Rosiek, 2007, p. 41).

This is very important. Other methodologies that view experience differently might begin with epistemological commitments (beliefs around how we know what we know) – with a theory or model to fit an individual's experiences into. The researcher in this case understands reality and experience as residing outside of an individual's experiences. It is imperative to understand how narrative inquir-ers' ontological commitments are quite different from other methodologies. This is because narrative inquirers view knowledge and understanding as residing in the eye of the beholder – the teacher, the professional – rather than in the eye of an external 'expert' or 'authority'. Furthermore, it is even more important to under-stand how this ontological commitment shapes a view of experience that drives each and every methodological decision made when using narrative inquiry.

Along with drawing on Dewey's pragmatic ontology, narrative inquirers also draw on Dewey's understanding of experiences. He understood that experiences are both *continuous* and *interactive* (Dewey, 1938). *Continuity* describes the temporal nature of experiences – they are shaped by time in that experiences build on other experiences and shape future experiences. *Interaction* describes the relational aspect of our experiences – they intermingle with the sociocultural environments and places in which we live. So, while our individual experiences are continuous, they are also constantly interacting with the places, people, and social environments within which we live.

> Framed within this view of experience, the focus of narrative inquiry is not only on individuals' experiences but also on the social, cultural, and institutional narratives within which individuals' experiences are constituted, shaped, expressed and enacted. Narrative inquirers study the individual's experience in the world, an experience that is storied both in living and tell-ing that can be studied by listening, observing, living alongside another and writing and interpreting texts.
>
> *(Clandinin & Rosiek, 2007, pp. 42–43)*

It is this understanding of experience that led Clandinin and Connelly (2000) to conceptualise the metaphorical three-dimensional narrative inquiry space.

Three-dimensional narrative inquiry space

When using narrative inquiry, experience is studied through explorations of the three 'common places.' Attending to these common places is one of the distinguishing features of narrative inquiry as compared to other narrative methodologies (Clandinin & Connelly, 2000). For example, as narrative inquirers engage with participants' stories, we ask questions which explore their (personal) feelings, hopes, and dispositions; the temporal (that is, how their experiences were bound in time); the social (that is, what was happening around them), and finally, place(s) (that is, the physical place in which an experience happens).

(a) *Common place of temporality.* The common place of temporality refers to the understanding that experience always has a past, present and future. Referring back to Dewey's (1938) understanding of experience we can see continuity and interaction as we think about how past experiences mesh with present experiences, which shape future experiences.

(b) *Common place of sociality.* The common place of sociality takes a perspective that while our own experiences are continuous, they are constantly interacting with the social conditions to which we belong. 'Social conditions refer to the milieu, the conditions under which people's experiences and events are unfolding' (Clandinin, 2013, p. 40). For example, as a beginning physical educator I experienced marginalisation. Attending to the larger social structures that position physical education as a discipline that is 'less than' helps to better understand how my experience was interacting with larger social conditions. Sociality also refers to personal conditions: 'we mean feelings, hopes, desires, aesthetic reactions and moral dispositions' (Connelly & Clandinin, 2006, p. 480) of the person. For example, noting that I felt marginalised means very little if you don't understand who I was and who I was becoming as a teacher. A third aspect of sociality 'directs attention to the inquiry relationship between researchers' and participants' lives. Narrative inquirers cannot subtract themselves from the inquiry relationship' (Huber & Clandinin, 2005, p. 4). This means that the interaction between researcher and participant is always part of the inquiry.

(c) *Common place of place.* The common place of place is quite literally the place in which the experience happens, 'which attends to the specific concrete physical and topological boundaries of inquiry landscapes' (Clandinin & Connelly, 2000, p. 51). Place is concerned with both the places where the inquiry happens, as well as the places that are storied within the participants' experiences. As an example, if an event takes place in a gymnasium space it is important to understand how that particular space may have shaped the experience.

Like the ontological commitment to experience, the three common places are also adhered to throughout the study. They help to design observations, conversations and potential field texts (data) collected throughout the study. As described in the above paragraph, the three dimensional space is also used to interpret and analyse the field texts with attention to temporality, sociality and place.

A relational methodology

In reading narrative inquiry studies you will soon notice that the word *relational* comes up often. Again, confusion can take place as readers make assumptions about this simply meaning that the researcher and participant build a relationship which allows for deeper inquiry. While each narrative inquiry is relational in some sense, they are not necessarily relational in the same ways. What we mean by that is the relationships that become apparent are different depending on the narrative inquirer, the participant and the process undertaken during the inquiry. While some narrative inquirers choose to 'live alongside' their participants, others choose to have conversations without living in the midst of the participants' lives. As Clandinin (2013, p. 23) notes, 'the relational' can include a variety of aspects:

> . . . the relation between the person and his/her world; a temporal understanding of the relational between past, present, and future, including the relational in the intergenerational; the relationship between persons and place; the relational between events and feelings; the relational between us as people; the relational between the physical world and people; the relational in our cultural, institutional, linguistic, and familial narratives . . .

Given the multiplicity of relational aspects that may influence a narrative inquiry, it becomes easy to see how narrative inquiries can take on quite different shapes and forms. For example, Clandinin and Connelly (2000) lived in a school for over three years alongside the teachers as they were engaged in a curriculum reform study. Similarly, Schaefer, Lessard and Lewis (2017) have been engaged in a narrative inquiry for over three years alongside urban Aboriginal youth, studying how the youth experience 'being well' in an after-school programme. Alternatively, Schaefer (2013) met with teachers outside of the school context and had conversations about how they experienced their first year as physical education teachers. Clandinin, Schaefer and Downey (2014) had conversations with early career teachers who left teaching in their first five years, and, in this case, it was impossible to live alongside them. Just from these examples, it becomes easy to see that the relational aspect of the inquiry vastly differs depending on the researchers, the participants, and the phenomenon being studied.

Justifying a narrative inquiry

While each narrative inquiry differs in regard to design, process, analysis and dissemination, Clandinin (2013) notes that each narrative inquiry should be justified in three ways to help answer the types of questions that arise as other scholars make decisions about the importance of a researcher's work.

(a) *Personal justification.* A personal justification is perhaps an aspect that situates narrative inquiry differently than other methodologies. Given the relational aspects of narrative inquiry, it is important that each researcher situates themselves within the study and within the phenomenon they are interested in. This often begins with autobiographical narrative inquiries that take into account the sociality, temporality and place of the researcher's experiences and how they relate to a particular phenomenon. For example, in our study into the experiences of early career teacher leavers, it was first important to inquire in to our own experiences of leaving teaching early, which included an autobiographical narrative inquiry into our experiences with coming to teaching, teaching and leaving teaching.

(b) *Practical justification.* Practical justifications are increasingly more important as granting agencies and academic journals ask researchers to explain how others will take up knowledge from their studies (i.e. how will others find it useful?). Clandinin (2013) sees this justification as asking questions about how your research will change practice. For example, using our study again into the experiences of early career leavers, policy and teacher induction programmes were shifted based on the findings from the study. Thus, practice was shifted because of this research. Teachers or coaches might also find that they can shift practice by sharing their findings with colleagues in a department, school, club or district.

(c) *Social justifications.* Social justifications can be conceptualised in two different ways (Clandinin, 2013). First, you could justify your study as shaping how we theoretically understand a particular phenomenon. Referring back to the study on early career leavers, we began to conceptualise early career teacher leaving as a phenomenon that could better be understood as a negotiation of identity, which has a rich theoretical background that we felt could help us make sense of what we were studying. Second, you could justify your work from a social action or policy perspective. Some may see this as emancipatory work that focuses on positive social change.

Looking back: a brief history of narrative and narrative inquiry

Bruner (2004), Martin (1986), Polkinghorne (1988), Sarbin (2004) and Clandinin and Connelly (2000) all extensively explore the emergence of narrative forms of knowledge and research. Reading each of their understandings of narrative forms of knowledge illustrates the breadth of understanding as well as the differing philosophical understanding of experience, story, narrative and research in general. As Clandinin (2006, p. 44) notes:

> As narrative inquirers look back on the rich meanings of the term narrative, there is now, however, a recognition that care must be taken in how we use

the terms 'narrative' and 'narrative inquiry'. As we undertake this careful delineation of terms, we realise how interwoven narrative ways of thinking about phenomena are with the ways that narrative methodologies are emerging.

While the scope of this chapter is not to delve into the complex nature of narrative, it is important for those interested in narrative inquiry to understand the multiple ways that narrative research and narrative inquiry are taken up. As mentioned at the beginning of this chapter, we are specifically looking here at narrative inquiry from Connelly and Clandinin's (1990) conception. Narrative inquiry (ibid.), like other research methods that use narrative, has continued to grow as the dominant discourses of research give way to multiple epistemological and ontological approaches of research. While the exact moment of this shift is unclear, a good starting point is Clandinin and Connelly's publication of their 1990 article 'Stories of experience and narrative inquiry' in *Educational Researcher*. *Educational Researcher* is one of the world's most prestigious educational research journals; it was (and still is) known for publishing mostly quantitative types of research. Therefore, Clandinin and Connelly publishing in this journal was a major historical point in narrative inquiry.

Clandinin and Connelly continued to work together for several decades (Clandinin & Connelly, 2000; Connelly & Clandinin, 2006) and they took up and published much of the early narrative inquiry research. Much of the research on the foundations of narrative inquiry published to date has been by Clandinin and Connelly or by their graduate students who worked with them.

As can be imagined, a large portion of the early published work was based around attempting to clearly define what narrative inquiry was and how it could be used as a method within educational research (Clandinin & Connelly, 1990, 1994, 2000). Given the shifting nature and emergence of new research methodologies, defining what narrative inquiry is, and is not, continues to be a major focus captured in the literature (Clandinin, 2006, 2013; Clandinin & Rosiek, 2007; Connelly & Clandinin, 2006; Downey & Clandinin, 2010).

Based on the philosophical implications of narrative inquiry and narrative inquiry as a methodology being conceptualised through studying teachers' knowledge, it should not be surprising that much of the early work focused on understanding teachers' knowledge and professional knowledge landscapes in narrative ways (Clandinin & Connelly, 1988, 1995, 1996). These studies led to seeing teachers as curriculum planners (Connelly & Clandinin, 1988), as well as narrative understandings of school reform, curriculum development and teacher education (Connelly & Clandinin, 1999; Clandinin, Downey, & Huber, 2009).

Clandinin and Connelly have worked alongside a number of graduate students over the years, which has led to a diverse use of narrative inquiry as a methodology. For example, Caine (2002) took up a visual narrative inquiry of Aboriginal women living with HIV, while Cardinal (2010) took up an autobiographical narrative inquiry that looked at her experiences as an Indigenous graduate student.

Young (2005) narratively inquired into how the loss of Aboriginal language is also a loss of identity. Schaefer (2013) worked with teachers who left the profession early, and Chan (2004) has used narrative inquiry to study how teachers explore culture within their classrooms through curriculum. Murphy (2004) inquired into elementary children's experiences of school to position children as knowledge holders. Lessard (2010) looked at the experiences of early school leavers to better understand both the language and policies that are aimed at high school students who leave before graduation. We list these studies to show the variety of topics that could be addressed by using narrative inquiry, but also to transition into how narrative inquiry has been used in physical education research.

Narrative inquiry in physical education

This section would be very short if we only included narrative inquiry studies around physical education completed using Connelly and Clandanin's (1990) original conception. Given the purpose of this book and the focus on physical education and youth sport, we find it useful to first, briefly, discuss the broad use of narrative research methods in physical education. We then move on more specifically to how narrative inquiry (ibid.) has emerged in physical education research.

A brief summary of narrative research in physical education

Dowling et al. (2014) and Armour (2006) provide extensive reviews that give a sense of both the variety of research questions and variety of data collection tools that have emerged through the use of narrative methodologies. Both authors allude to the fact that narrative research still resides on the boundaries of preferred methods used in physical education research. While prospective teachers and researchers may be wary to take up methodologies that don't fit the dominant perspective of what counts as research (i.e. typically quantitative, generalisable), the emergence of narrative research specifically attempts to disrupt dominant ways of doing research. In fact, the history of narrative research in physical education began because 'there was a growing dissatisfaction with an overreliance on the empirical-analytical paradigm, which had rendered teachers to statistics in large scale surveys and interactionist and anthropological studies which focused mainly upon classrooms and cast teachers as seemingly interchangeable' (Dowling et al. 2014, p. 3).

When the terms *narrative* and *physical education* are mentioned together, historically, Andrew Sparkes's name was present. Sparkes's (1992, 1995, 2002; Sparkes et al. 1993) work with narrative in physical education bumped against the dominant ways of doing physical education research; perhaps this is why so many others, since then, have come to see narrative research as offering new ways to engage with both traditional and contemporary phenomena in physical education

(Dowling et al., 2014). While Dowling et al. (ibid.) and Armour (2006) do well to summarise the impact of narrative methods in physical education, there is little to go on in regard to how one might take up narrative methods in physical education or youth sport, or how the differing philosophical views of narrative researchers drastically shifts how research is taken up.

Narrative inquiry in physical education

In regard to narrative inquiry from Clandinin and Connelly's (1990) conception, there has been very little work done within physical education. Recently, Craig, You and Oh (2012) used narrative inquiry to study the intersection between teachers and curriculum. These authors also looked at how narrative inquiry provides a meaningful methodology to study physical education classroom settings, as well as how physical educators might become teachers as curriculum makers. In both cases the authors found that narrative inquiry provided a meaningful methodology to better understand the lived experiences of those individuals engaged in physical education.

Schaefer's (2013) research looked at how using narrative inquiry as a research methodology has in turn shaped his pedagogy as a physical education teacher educator. In an autobiographical way, he showed how the common places (temporality, sociality and place) as well as Dewey's notion of experience had begun to shape his course outlines, assignments, and relationships with students. In a similar vein, Gleddie and Schaefer (2014) used autobiographical narrative inquiry to explore how the common places of narrative inquiry were indeed shaping who they were as PETE educators. In better understanding how their experiences had shaped their pedagogy they became more critical about how their own experiences may marginalise the experiences of those who had negative experiences with physical education and physical activity. Both authors are currently working on a narrative inquiry into how using autobiographical work with PETE pre-service teachers may also help them to think more about equity and diversity within physical education.

Schaefer & Clandinin (2011) used narrative inquiry to explore the experiences of two beginning physical education teachers and found that sustaining themselves in teaching was much more complex than what was currently in the early career teacher attrition literature. For example, attending to their imagined stories of teaching helped them to better understand how they may be sustained as teachers. Casey and Schaefer (2014) used narrative inquiry to explore a beginning physical education teacher's tensions as his imagined stories of teaching physical education bumped with the dominant stories of physical education at the school he was teaching. Casey and Schaefer (2014) ended with making a justification for the use of narrative inquiry as both a research methodology and as a way to think about preparing future physical educators whose stories to live by will no doubt bump with the stories of the professional knowledge landscapes they enter in to. Christensen (2012) also used narrative inquiry to explore how beginning physical education teachers negotiate the micro-political staffroom stories that were present in the physical education staffroom. She found that narrative inquiry offered new knowledge that had implications for policy, as well as teacher induction and transition.

Future possibilities of narrative inquiry in physical education and sport

At this potentially transformational time there is no doubt that questions of 'whose knowledge' and 'who gains' and the micro-, meso- and macro-politics at work will expand and continue to invite multiple understandings of physical education. We have new (or renewed) questions about the role of PETE in developing new orientations to physical education, such as joy (Blankenship & Ayers, 2010; Gleddie & Schaefer, 2014), social justice (Robinson & Randall, 2016) and the meaning of being a lifelong mover (Kretchmar, 2008). These shifting orientations offer other ways for researchers to understand how PETE research impacts teaching, teacher education, and perhaps society.

Given the infancy of narrative inquiry's use in physical education, it is hard to anticipate what the future holds. From our experience working alongside graduate students as well as other colleagues using narrative inquiry, the methodology seems to offer something new and powerful in ways that we understand experience and teacher knowledge. While narrative inquiry has predominantly been used by teacher educators, a brief look at the narrative inquiry landscape shows that studies of curriculum, student knowledge, teacher knowledge, physical activity dispositions, experiences with marginality, and so on could be further explored using this methodology, offering new insights and understanding of the field.

Positioning the emphasis upon the participants, whether they be teacher educators, teachers, or students, provides an opportunity to focus on experiences, as opposed to theoretical frames that have often been used in physical education and health research. This focus on experience gives value to participants' voices, includes them in the research in meaningful ways, and perhaps offers new ways to bring about different and deep understanding of teaching and learning going forward. It is our hope that the narrative inquiry chapter in the following part (see Chapter 7) might provide further insight into how you might use narrative inquiry to explore your phenomenon of choice.

References

Armour, K. (2006). The way to a teacher's heart: Narrative research in physical education. In D. Kirk, D. Macdonald & M. O'Sullivan (eds), *Handbook of physical education* (pp. 467–485). London: Sage Publications.

Blankenship, B. T., & Ayers, S. F. (2010). The role of PETE in developing joy-oriented physical educators. *Quest, 62*(2), 171–183.

Bruner, J. (2004). Life as narrative. *Social Research*, *71*(3), 691–710.

Caine, V. (2002). Storied moments: A visual narrative inquiry of aboriginal women living with HIV. Unpublished master's thesis, University of Alberta, Edmonton, Alberta, Canada.

Cardinal, T. (2010). For all my relations: An autobiographical narrative inquiry into the lived experiences of one Aboriginal graduate student. Unpublished master's thesis, University of Alberta, Edmonton, Alberta, Canada.

Casey, A. & Schaefer, L. (2016). A narrative inquiry into the negotiation of the dominant stories of physical education: Living, telling, re-telling and re-living. *Sport Education and Society*, *21*(1), 114–130.

Chan, E. (2004). Narratives of ethnic identity: Experiences of first generation Chinese Canadian students. Unpublished doctoral dissertation, Ontario Institute for Studies in Education of the University of Toronto, Toronto, Canada.

Christensen, E. (2012). Micropolitical staffroom stories: Beginning health and physical education teachers' experiences of the staffroom. *Teaching and Teacher Education*, *30*, 74–83.

Clandinin, D.J. (2006). Narrative inquiry: A methodology for studying lived experience. *Research Studies in Music Education*, *27*(1), 44–54.

Clandinin, D.J. (2013). *Engaging in narrative inquiry*. London: Routledge.

Clandinin, D.J., & Connelly, F.M. (1988). *Teachers as curriculum planners: Narratives of experience*. New York: Teachers College Press.

Clandinin, D.J., & Connelly, F.M. (1994). Personal experience methods. In N.K. Denzin & Y.S. Lincoln (eds), *Handbook of qualitative research* (pp. 413–427). Thousand Oaks, CA: Sage.

Clandinin, D.J., & Connelly, F.M. (1995). *Teachers' professional knowledge landscapes*. New York: Teachers College Press.

Clandinin, D.J., & Connelly, F.M. (1996). Teachers' professional knowledge landscapes: Teacher stories – stories of teachers – school stories – stories of school. *Educational Researcher*, *25*(3), 24–30.

Clandinin, D.J., & Connelly, F.M. (2000). *Narrative inquiry: Experience and story in qualitative research*. San Francisco, CA: Jossey-Bass.

Clandinin, D.J., Downey, C.A., & Huber, J. (2009). Attending to changing landscapes: Shaping the interwoven identities of teachers and teacher educators. *Asia-Pacific Journal of Teacher Education*, *37*(2), 141–154.

Clandinin, D.J., & Huber, M. (2005). Shifting stories to live by: Interweaving the personal and professional in teacher's lives. In D. Beijaard, P.C. Meijer, G. Morine-Dershimer & H. Tillema (eds), *Teacher professional development in changing conditions* (pp. 43–59). Dordrecht: Springer.

Clandinin, D.J., Huber, J., Huber, M., Murphy, S., Orr, A.M., Pearce, M., & Steeves, P. (2006). *Composing diverse identities: Narrative inquiries into the interwoven lives of children and teachers*. New York: Routledge.

Clandinin, D.J. & Rosiek, J. (2007). Mapping a landscape of narrative inquiry: Borderland spaces and tensions. In D.J. Clandinin (ed.), *Handbook of narrative inquiry: Mapping a methodology* (pp. 35–75). London: Sage.

Clandinin, D.J., Schaefer, L., & Downey, A. (2014). *Narrative conceptions of knowledge: Towards understanding teacher attrition*. London: Emerald Publishing.

Connelly, F.M., & Clandinin, D.J. (1988). *Teachers as curriculum planners: Narratives of experience*. New York: Teachers College Press.

Connelly, F.M., & Clandinin, D.J. (1990). Stories of experience and narrative inquiry. *Educational Researcher*, *19*(5), 2–14.

Connelly, F.M., & Clandinin, D.J. (1999). Knowledge, context and identity: Shaping a professional identity: Stories of educational practice, 1–5.

Connelly, F.M., & Clandinin, D.J. (2006). Narrative inquiry. In J.L. Green, G. Camilli, P. Elmore (eds), *Handbook of complementary methods in education research* (3rd ed., pp. 477–487). Mahwah, NJ: Lawrence Erlbaum.

Craig, C., You, J., & Oh, S. (2012). Why school-based narrative inquiry in physical education research? An international perspective. *Asia Pacific Journal of Education, 32*(3), 271–284.

Dewey, J. (1938). *Experience and education.* New York: Collier Books.

Dowling, F., Garrett, R., Hunter, L., & Wrench, A. (2014). Narrative inquiry in physical education research: The story so far. *Sport, Education and Society, 20*(7), 924–940.

Downey, C.A., & Clandinin, D.J. (2010). Narrative inquiry as reflective practice: Tensions and possibilities. In N. Lyons (ed.), *Handbook of reflection and reflective inquiry* (pp. 383–397). New York: Springer.

Gleddie, D., & Schaefer, L. (2014). Autobiographical narrative inquiry into movement and physical education: The beginning of a journey. *PHEnex Journal, 6*(3), 1–14.

Huber, J., & Clandinin, D.J. (2005). Living in tension: Negotiating a curriculum of lives on the professional knowledge landscape. In J. Brophy & S. Pinnegar (eds), *Learning from research on teaching: Perspective, methodology, and representation* (pp. 313–336). Bingley: Emerald Group Publishing.

Kretchmar, R.S. (2008). The increasing utility of elementary school physical education: A mixed blessing and unique challenge. *The Elementary School Journal, 108*(3), 161–170.

Lessard, S. (2010) Red worn runners: A narrative inquiry into the stories of aboriginal youth and families in urban settings. Unpublished doctoral dissertation, University of Alberta, Edmonton, Alberta, Canada.

Martin, W. (1986). *Recent theories of narrative.* Ithaca, NY: Cornell University Press.

Murphy, M.S. (2004). Understanding children's knowledge: A narrative inquiry into school experiences. Unpublished doctoral dissertation, University of Alberta, Edmonton, Alberta, Canada.

Pinnegar, S. & Daynes, J. (2007). Locating narrative inquiry historically. In D.J. Clandinin (ed.), *Handbook of narrative inquiry: Mapping a methodology* (pp. 1–34). Thousand Oaks, CA: Sage.

Polkinghorne, D. (1988). *Narrative knowing and the human sciences.* New York: State University of New York Press.

Robinson, D., & Randall, L. (2016). *Social justice in physical education: Critical reflection and pedagogies for change.* Vancouver: Canadian Scholars Press.

Sarbin, T.R. (2004). The role of imagination in narrative construction. In C. Daiute & C. Lightfoot (eds), *Narrative analysis: Studying the development of individuals in society* (pp. 5–20). Thousand Oaks, CA: Sage.

Schaefer, L. (2013). Narrative inquiry for physical education pedagogy. *International Journal of Pedagogies and Learning, 8*(1), 18–26.

Schaefer, L., & Clandinin, D.J. (2011). A narrative inquiry into beginning teachers' experiences. *LEARNing Landscapes, 4*(2), 275–296.

Schaefer, L., Lessard, S., & Lewis, B. (2017). Living tensions of co-creating a wellness program and narrative inquiry alongside urban aboriginal youth. *LEARNing Landscapes.*

Sparkes, A. (1992). *Research in physical education and sport: Exploring alternative visions.* London: Falmer Press.

Sparkes, A.C. (1995). Writing people: Reflections on the dual crises of representation and legitimation in qualitative inquiry. *Quest, 47*(2), 158–195.

Sparkes, A. C. (2002). *Telling tales in sport and physical activity*. Champaign, IL: Human Kinetics.

Sparkes, A. C., Templin, T. J., & Schempp, P. G. (1993). Exploring dimensions of marginality: Reflecting on the life histories of physical education teachers. *Journal of Teaching in Physical Education*, *12*(4), 386–398.

Young, M. (2005). Pimatisiwin: Walking in a good way. A narrative inquiry into language as identity. Unpublished doctoral dissertation, University of Alberta, Edmonton, Alberta, Canada.

4

AUTOETHNOGRAPHY

Introduction

This chapter explores the nuances of ethnography and delves deeply into one of its sub-fields, autoethnography. Ethnography has a storied and somewhat controversial past rooted in anthropology. In its early conception, ethnography involved anthropologists going into the field, living with their 'subjects', and observing cultural practices as found in the subjects' day-to-day lives. The scientists would then leave to write completely unbiased and objective reports about the strange and weird practices of an unfamiliar culture. The illusion of objectivity was shattered when the wife of prominent anthropologist Bronislaw Malinowski posthumously released his field diaries as a book: *A Diary in the Strict Sense of the Term* (Malinowski, 1989). As renowned ethnographer Clifford Geertz put it:

> Most of the shock seems to have arisen from the mere discovery that Malinowski was not, to put it delicately, an unmitigated nice guy. He had rude things to say about the natives he was living with and rude words to say it in. He spent a great deal of his time wishing he were elsewhere.
>
> *(Geertz, 1975, p. 47)*

Ethnographers began to be more conscious of their own role and position in the research they were conducting, questioning and challenging the accepted *emic* (subject) and *etic* (observer) perspectives.

More recently, ethnography has contributed to the sphere of qualitative research methodology with such iterations as critical ethnography (1960s) based in Marxist or neo-Marxist theory and questioning positivist notions of objectivity rooted in colonialism (Foley, Valenzuela, Denzin & Lincoln, 2005). From the critical ethnographic traditions, autoethnography emerged (perhaps quite naturally) as a form of studying the self whereby the text is written from the retrospective viewpoint of a person interpreting his or her own past (Ellis, 2004; Ellis & Bochner, 2000; Vone'che, 2001).

The purpose of this chapter is to provide an overview of autoethnography in general, then narrow to its place in youth sport and physical education. Therefore, we will begin with the broader educational applications of autoethnography (Hamdan, 2012) and move to a narrow look at the development of the genre in sport and physical education (Purdy, Potrac, & Jones, 2008; Sparkes, 2002). The chapter will then introduce the limited but growing literature of autoethnographic physical education and youth sport focused research (Cameron, 2012; Carless, 2012; McParland, 2013; Morimoto, 2008). Finally, we will explore future directions for using autoethnography as a tool for the reflective practitioner in physical education and youth sport.

What is autoethnography?

> autoethnography is not simply a way of knowing about the world; it has become a way of being in the world, one that requires living consciously, emotionally, and reflexively. It asks that we not only examine our lives but also consider how and why we think, act and feel as we do. Autoethnography requires that we observe ourselves observing, that we interrogate what we think and believe, and that we challenge our own assumptions, asking over and over if we have penetrated as many layers of our own defences, fears and insecurities as our project requires.
>
> (Ellis, in Holman Jones, Adams, & Ellis, 2016, p. 10)

Autoethnography is a qualitative methodology designed to examine or describe (*graphy*) the self (*auto*) in the context of culture (*ethno*). It emerged quite naturally out of ethnography (Ellis, 1993; Ellis & Bochner, 1996) partially as a reaction to prevailing colonialist, positivist, modernist standpoints in the field of anthropology. These modernist standpoints have been criticised for privileging and prioritising western views as well as offering a perception of objectivity represented by numbers and research in the quantitative sphere. Along with other advances in qualitative methodology, autoethnography represents a shift in the social sciences to embrace stories and subjectivity rather than theories and objectivity. Although methodologies such as narrative inquiry and self-study of practice also embrace story and subjectivity through personalised writing processes, one aspect that distinguishes autoethnography from these other approaches is the researcher's connection to culture (Ellis, Adams, & Bochner, 2011).

What are the main features of autoethnography?

According to Chang (2008) autoethnography rests on four foundational assumptions.

1   Culture by its very nature involves groups – the individual is always connected to others. In this way, we need to pay attention to the relationships

surrounding the individual, such as those that involve family, peers, authorities and societal structures.

2   Reading and writing autoethnography allows viewing and understanding both self and others. As we write about ourselves, or read about individuals, the purpose is first to listen and learn, then to seek understanding.

3   Telling a story does not immediately equal cultural understanding. In order to begin to comprehend the self and other in culture, we need to take time for deep cultural analysis, discourse and interpretation. Understanding culture and the relationships therein is a process that takes time and effort.

4   Autoethnography is a method of teaching. Studies can be used to assist the development of cultural understanding and therefore lead to more effective relationships and societal functions.

Holman Jones et al. (2016) have provided a conceptualisation of autoethnography that further distinguishes the methodology from other forms of self-narrative (e.g. autobiography). In their interpretation, there are four key distinguishing characteristics (Table 4.1).

As a subset of autoethnography it may be helpful for practitioners in sport and physical education to understand aspects and procedures of *collaborative*

TABLE 4.1 Four key characteristics of autoethnography (quotations taken from Holman Jones, Adams & Ellis, 2016).

Characteristic	*Explanation*
'purposefully commenting on/ critiquing of culture and cultural practices' (p. 22)	Writing that uses stories to share experiences but does *not* analyse the story in the explicit cultural context is *autobiography*. Autoethnography illustrates cultural phenomena and can provide voice and story for those normally overlooked or ignored.
'making contributions to existing research' (p. 22)	Autoethnography recognises knowledge and understanding from other research in a pertinent topic. Previous findings are not ignored but rather can be explored and often challenged (see section above). The methodology contributes to the scholarly knowledge as well as general audiences.
'embracing vulnerability with purpose' (p. 22)	The 'auto' aspect of the method invites an openness so as to share personal experience. '[A]uthors purposefully open themselves up to "the possibility of being wounded or attacked" in order to call attention to the vulnerabilities that other human beings may endure in silence or in shame' (p. 24, quoting Behar, 1998).
'creating a reciprocal relationship with audiences in order to compel a response' (p. 22)	Autoethnography intends to both begin and continue conversations of the shared experience featured. Audiences are treated as active, not passive.

autoethnography. Collaborative autoethnography may be useful in our field because coaching and teaching are never done in isolation. While it can be effective to examine one's own story – alone – there are other cases where working collaboratively can be more effective (such as Chapter 8). According to Chang, Wambura Ngunjiri and Hernandez (2013), there are numerous ways to engage in autoethnography in a *collaborative* fashion (which may seem anathema to the idea of 'auto'). The number of collaborating members can vary from two person teams to three person teams or (in rare cases) even more members. As well, collaborative autoethnography can extend to full collaboration, where all members of the research team share equal roles and responsibilities (Kalmbach Phillips et al., 2009; Geist-Martin et al., 2010). Full collaboration stands in contrast to partial collaboration that includes a range of engagement from the research team regarding the sharing of autobiographical data, researching, analysing and writing. Finally, there are also variations in the methodology to include: autoethnographic conversations, community autoethnography, duoethnography and performance collaborative autoethnography. For those readers that are interested in learning more about these advanced approaches to autoethnography, we recommend an entire book on the topic: *Collaborative Autoethnography* (Chang et al., 2013).

To further understand what makes autoethnography a viable choice for practitioner inquiry in sport and physical education, there is a need to be aware of the purposes of the methodology. In other words, it is important for the practitioner researcher to understand the circumstances and contexts, benefits and nuances that exist for a teacher or coach to use autoethnography to explore their experience in relation to culture. Holman Jones et al. (2016) suggest five key purposes that serve to make autoethnography both unique and compelling:

1   *Disrupting norms.* The sharing of deep experience required of the methodology serves to upset established norms, particularly in the ways research is conducted and represented. As you will see later, the history of autoethnography is rooted in exactly this disruption of positivist, 'scientific' ways of knowing and ways of sharing. A recognition that research can be more than randomised control trials is related to the awareness that sharing of research can look like poetry or performance. This can also serve to make research more enticing or engaging to readers. Early in its emergence, autoethnographic researchers spent inordinate amounts of time defending the methodology in trying to get their work published (acknowledged) due to the established norms and predominant discourses of the research community (see, for example, Holt, 2003).

2   *Insider knowledge.* This is what distinguishes autoethnography from ethnography, where researchers traditionally sought to: (a) infiltrate a cultural group to become an accepted part of a community, (b) observe and record, and (c) leave and write about the culture – often never to return again. In autoethnography, the research topic is experience itself and is therefore inherently personal. As a result, autoethnographic research can include some extremely personal and

sometimes painful topics written subjectively by those living with or inside the phenomenon: being a 'fat' physical education instructor (Morimoto, 2008); same-sex attraction in school sport (Carless, 2012); perceptions of teacher identity and efficacy of a 'crippled' physical education teacher (Fisette, 2013); and the negotiation of gender stereotypes with a female basketball player (McParland, 2013).

3   *Moving through difficulties to make life better.* Many autoethnographic studies begin with feelings of confusion, neglect, anger or conflict. The process of data gathering, writing, analysis and writing can be cathartic while at the same time painful. Researchers are often seeking insights and answers for themselves during difficult experiences, in their past, present and future. However, auto-ethnography also offers a chance to make life better through both formal and informal processes of publication or performance. This can occur in several ways: through the sharing of personal struggles and experiences that are unique ('Oh wow, I had no idea – I understand the situation better now'); through a sense of relatedness and insight ('I had a similar experience of sexism, now I have some coping tools'); and through a sense of living with each other's stories ('We can make our lives and others' lives better when we learn from each other's experiences').

4   *Breaking silence, claiming voice, 'writing' wrongs.* Connected with and flowing from the purposes above, autoethnography serves to bring to light individual experience within and through cultures and practices. Each of the authors noted in point 2 above had a unique personal experience within a cultural setting and sought to give themselves and others (often hidden, suppressed or neglected within the particular culture) a voice and some volume. Sometimes, these authors also hope to 'write to right' (Bolen, 2012) the wrongs they perceive within the particular cultural context and bring about positive change through sharing their experiences with others.

5   *Accessibility of the work.* Let's face it – most practitioners do not read research. And why should they? Highly theoretical, full of big words and jargon, not to mention being published in journals that are expensive and inaccessible to most teachers and coaches. The final purpose for autoethnography as a methodology is to make research findings accessible to a variety of audiences. This does not mean the work is not academic or rigorous, it just means that the format, media and venues tend to be more open and available than many other traditional forms of research.

As we get down to actually 'doing the work' of autoethnography there are some common understandings that guide the processes and procedures for this type of research. Adams, Holman Jones and Ellis (2015) have identified six key issues linked to engaging in quality autoethnographic research:

• *Foregrounding personal experience*: as illustrated earlier, as opposed to positivist research, autoethnography allows for and firmly embraces the need for personal narratives to be the subject of both research and writing. Researchers in this field choose to research and write about their own private experiences within cultural settings. This work is primarily motivated in three, often interconnected ways: (a) feelings, attitudes and beliefs about an experience, (b) issues of identity, and (c) epiphanies.

- *Making sense*: autoethnography involves a process of trying to understand particular cultural practices from an individual perspective. These personal interactions and sense making processes can provide direction and insight to others trying to figure out a similar experience (racism, cancer, bullying).
- *Reflexivity*: researchers in this area continually circle back to the past to understand the present and plan for the future. Cause and effect are interrelated and embedded in cultural norms, practices and experiences.
- *Insider cultural knowledge*: autoethnography allows for an 'epistemology of insiderness' (Buzard, cited in Adams et al., 2015, p. 31) that is unavailable to researchers coming in from the 'outside'. For example, someone suffering from a critical illness or disorder can offer a personal insight that would never be encompassed by a medical study or interview protocol.
- *Describing and critiquing culture*: stemming from the insider perspective, autoethnographers play a critical role in both describing and critiquing cultural norms and practices. The description, because it is internal and personal, has the capability for 'thickness' and 'richness'. Cultural critique comes from a desire to seek understanding, challenge accepted norms and facilitate social discussion and change.
- *Audience response*: autoethnography is relational and responsive, seeking to engage readers in a socially conscious act of reflection. Participants, researchers and audiences are drawn into a process of reciprocal responding through participation and relationship.

A brief history of autoethnography

As stated earlier, the roots of autoethnography lie in ethnography and anthropology. Historically, there were four primary trends that led to the growth of this method (Holman et al., 2016). First, there has been a growing respect for and engagement in qualitative research and the recognition that scientific knowledge (positivist) has limitations. Qualitative methodologies can allow for a range of human experience unconstrained by predictability and stability (Denzin & Lincoln, 2000). Therefore, these types of methodologies and their methods tend to be used to examine the unique aspects and experiences of individuals or particular cultures.

Second, researchers were becoming increasingly concerned with the ethical implications and consequences of research involving human subjects (participants). Projects such as the Tuskegee Syphilis Study, where subjects were taken from marginalised populations and in some cases denied treatment in the name of 'science', led to guidelines and ethical principles involving respect, beneficence and justice (e.g. the Belmont Report in the USA). These ethical concerns and guidelines from the quantitative realm also led to qualitative questioning of issues such as representation, voice and perceptions (Chapter 11 deals more explicitly with the ethical implications of all four of the methodologies).

Third, stemming from the above issues of representation, there was a realisation that research projects consciously absented narrative, emotion, embodiment and aesthetics: 'consider what social sciences would become if they were closer to literature than physics, if they proffered stories rather than theories, and if they were self-consciously value-centred rather than pretending to be value-free' (Ellis et al., 2011, p. 274). Finally, autoethnography began to be recognised as a way to research and interpret social identities and the interaction with a broad definition of culture. Gender, sexual orientation, race, class and religion are all predominantly featured and offer a myriad of assumptions, voices, values and beliefs that disrupt and question the dominant discourse (ibid.).

How autoethnography has been used in professional settings

The key purposes of autoethnography (Holman Jones et al., 2016) make it an ideal form of inquiry within a variety of professional settings. Let's examine three categories of examples:

- *Insider knowledge.* Within the medical field, autoethnography is gaining credence due to the ability to share unique and specialised knowledge. Farrell, Bourgeois-Law, Regehr and Ajjawi (2015) argue that medical educators can benefit from the study of self, embedded in culture. Through this type of work, a better understanding of cultures and practices within the field can be gained. In criminology, Wakeman (2014) argues that autoethnography can help criminologists come to a deeper understanding of users, addiction and drug culture. Although the methodology is not some sort of magic formula, a deeper consideration of humanity through life history and experiences of self is needed within criminology.
- *Breaking silence/claiming voice.* Hernandez, Wabbura Ngunjiri and Chang (2015) give voice to immigrant women of colour working in higher education. They share their particular viewpoint as a resource for others in their shoes to advocate and advance within universities. In the criminal justice area, an autoethnographic perspective from former prisoners has been argued to add depth and colour to research in the field (Newbold, Ross, Jones, Richards, & Lenza, 2014). The authors posit that prison research has become too data driven and impersonal; therefore, research by former convicts who are now academics bringing their insider voices is beneficial.
- *Accessibility of research.* Through collaboration with faculty and mentor teachers in a 'third space', Taylor, Klein and Abrams (2014) identify and work through tensions in their own teacher education programme. They share their process for the purposes of enhancing other field-based teacher education programmes. Similarly, Ai (2016) uses autoethnography to explore a personal and cultural process of learning and teaching English as a foreign language in China. Ai

proposes a pedagogy based on the work and encourages others to consider the learning for their own practices in teaching and learning English.

How autoethnography has been used in physical education and youth sport

Researching sport and physical education through autoethnography, although still not common, seems to be on a slight rise over the last decade and a half. In this section we provide a short overview within the field of key/selected autoethnographic papers examining topics of study and critical learnings. These papers fall into several broad categories: coaches/coaching, athletes, teachers, and physical education teacher education (PETE).

Purdy et al. (2008) used autoethnography to explore the dynamics between a coach and an athlete in competitive rowing – from an athlete's perspective. They chose this methodology as a way to document the complex power relationships within elite sport. Using a distinct time period (six months), memories, diary entries and emails, the authors constructed inter-related stories to explore the culture of elite sport and the roles of those within. In their conclusion, they recognise both the strengths and limitations of autoethnography in this type of relationship and hope others can learn from their work by exploring the power dynamic that exists between coaches and athletes. In another coaching related autoethnography, this time from the perspective of the coach, Mills (2015) focuses on identity formation. His research follows a time of transition (return to coaching) within a coaching career in football (soccer) and includes the death of his father (friend, coach and mentor), time away from coaching and the journey to come back. In his words, 'it is also hoped that this narrative may provide support to other coaches and bind those who share similar experiences together to tell their collective stories' (ibid., p. 616). The final coaching article strays a little from what we have seen thus far and uses 'ethnodrama' as a form of autoethnography. Cassidy, Kidman and Dudfield (2015) created a script to provide insight into one coach director's experience of creating a coach development programme to align with New Zealand's *Coach Development Framework*. Interviews, informal discussions, field notes and critical incidences were used to produce a non-fiction script that tells the story in a creative and unique way. Although the authors found that performance art was an effective way to stimulate discussion and provoke thought, there were limitations – especially presenting the ethnodrama in a 'traditional' academic conference venue.

The athletes' voice has also been featured in the literature. Carless (2012) uses autoethnography to delve into his experiences of negotiating homosexuality and masculinity within the realm of school sport. He shares his story as a response to the lack of research and visibility of gay males in sport and physical education – especially within adolescent school sport. Carless offers his work 'in the hope that it might increase understanding of other same-sex attracted young males in sport' (ibid., p. 622). McParland (2013) explores conceptions of gender through a unique paper written as four 'quarters' of a basketball game. Beginning with historical restrictions on women in sport, she then moves through her childhood, university experience and a concluding section that incorporates all three – each exploring gender roles, athletes and sport. In her conclusion she urges, 'Get off the bench, women, and write your own rules' (ibid., p. 34)!

Brooks and Dinan Thompson (2015) use autoethnography to share insider knowledge of what it is like to be an elementary physical education specialist. Their study takes place over a three-year span and seeks to begin a discussion of how the elementary physical education specialist is perceived – in both place and space. The authors found a sense of 'placelessness' embedded in the social and cultural practices of elementary schools. Lack of contact with other teachers, limited professional development and isolated teaching resulted in feelings of exclusion. However, the authors also state, 'I look back and reflect fondly on my three years at one school. That time has given me the knowledge, support and motivation to be an activist' (p. 336). Also a physical educator, Fisette (2013) challenges the common discourse of able-bodied physical education teachers. She explores her initial teacher identity that was rooted in athleticism and ability, then is forced to re-examine herself as a physical educator after a spinal injury, multiple surgeries and partial paralysis. Fisette takes us on a journey from ability to disability and back to ability again. She challenges us to (re)consider who and what physical education teachers are and can be:

> Do any other physical educators have a stigma like me and question their ability to teach, to lead by example? I challenge you to come forward. I challenge you to expose your stigma and share your identity with us. Then, maybe, just maybe, if you come forward, my Scarlett Letter can disappear. And, even more importantly, we, together, can take down the traditional, hegemonic, socially constructed ideal of what it means to be a physical educator.
>
> *(Fisette, 2013, p. 484)*

The largest body of autoethnographic work in our field of study can be found in PETE (Cameron, 2012; Holmes, 2015; Legge, 2014; Morimoto, 2008; Sparkes, Brown & Partington, 2007, 2010). Although ethnographic in nature, the work of Sparkes, Brown and Partington (2007, 2010) helped to set the groundwork for connecting personal and cultural studies within the teacher education field. Their conceptualisation of 'jock culture' in PETE is regularly cited in autoethnographic works and includes elements of embodiment, ability, space and hegemony. Morimoto (2008), like Fisette (2013) and McParland (2013) earlier, challenges dominant discourses in physical education. For her, as a 'fat physical education instructor', the discourses include both ability and embodiment. Her writing is achingly poignant as she draws the reader into her world using poetry, prose and sound argument. Her opening poem includes the lines:

> This girl is fat . . . And surprise! She teaches PE. She frequently faces a sea of skeptical eyes that try to envision a fat dance yoga football teacher or even, a

fat sport history or sociology professor. But dancing a Viennese waltz with a fat girl makes a person re-think what fat is or is not . . .

(Morimoto, 2008, p. 29)

Cameron (2012) uses autoethnography to study her construction of identity and her journey as a PETE scholar. She asks the key question, 'What informs and continues to inform the athlete–student–teacher I am?' (ibid., p. 2). Cameron answers her question using reflexive journals, classroom experiences and scholarly dialogue to share her story. She embraces her own story to better understand those of her students and their acts of resistance in regard to critical pedagogy. She argues that PETE instructors need more strategies to engage students (and themselves) in negotiating the dominant discourses in meaningful and reflexive ways. In a complementary fashion, Maureen Legge (2014) writes about her eleven-year journey as a PETE instructor within the Māori (Indigenous) and Pākehā (European) cultures. Her work illustrates her efforts to integrate Māori culture into her role as a teacher educator – an insider view from the Pākehā perspective. 'Through writing I negotiated research terrain where the personal, the professional, the political, the social, and the cultural were juxtaposed against the other so that similarities and differences intersected, overlapped or clashed with one another' (ibid., p. 130). Hard work indeed, but also necessary.

The possibilities of autoethnography in physical education and youth sport

As can be seen from the previous section, there are numerous opportunities for the effective use of autoethnography in physical education and youth sport. To explore this potential, albeit briefly, let's return to the purposes of autoethnography as defined earlier by Holman Jones et al. (2016) and apply these to our chosen field.

1 Disrupting norms: as can be seen by the work of Carless (2012) and Fisette (2013), autoethnography is effective in challenging the dominant and encouraging reflexive contemplation – even action. Those in sport and physical education who wish to consider their position or role in the ongoing discourses regarding gender, ethnicity and ability (to name a few) may find a platform in autoethnography. As well, this method may provide leverage to share stories and reflect on people's differing experiences in a particular culture. For example, how does a physical education teacher who values meaningful movement and joy (Kretchmar, 2008) struggle with their values and identities in a pedagogical culture where a focus on 'fixing' childhood obesity seems to be the norm?

2 Insider knowledge: to some extent, each of us has some form of insider knowledge as our stories and experiences with and within culture are unique. When

considering autoethnography as practitioner research, it is important to ask what pieces of knowledge and experience can be shared that will benefit those within and without my circumstances. Jodi's work in Chapter 8 is certainly valuable to other mothers who are physical education teachers. However, her perspective is also important to those who are NOT in her shoes as her story can resonate to fathers, those without children, etc.

3   Moving through difficulties to make life better: Morimoto's (2008) article is a classic example of fighting through strife for the purpose of improving life. Whether the strife is 'fat shaming', gender stereotypes (McParland, 2013) or 'jock culture' (Sparkes, Brown, & Partington, 2007, 2010), stories and experiences are shared to improve life for the writer – and others. Consider what difficulties you have had to face and what can be learned from the struggle.

4   Breaking silence, claiming voice, 'writing' wrongs: we know that physical education and youth sport are fields that continue to struggle with, for example, a culture of sexism and gender stereotypes. Autoethnography can provide a way to voice an alternative experience; share what has not been shared before; and begin a discussion that will hopefully result in righting some of what is wrong within our profession. Shedding light on hurtful and sexist practices within sport (i.e. the hiring of predominantly male coaches and athletic directors) and physical education (i.e. dance is for girls, wrestling is for boys) can bring about change.

5   Accessibility of the work: autoethnography is readable, relatable and, through its variety of forms (McParland, 2013; Morimoto, 2008), is imminently accessible. The methodology is meant to be shared with a wider audience than 'just researchers'. Consider how your story can be shared, and with whom. What audience is best? What media allows for the power of your experience to come through?

To conclude, autoethnography provides a venue and methodology for personal and professional learning. Personal introspection and analysis in a cultural context (defined broadly) is difficult, but necessary work. Through autoethnography, we can explore concepts of the 'culture' of physical education and sport from our personal experience with the dual goals of sharing more widely and making a change for the better.

Further reading and resources

A number of key texts and resources are available to provide further guidance and a deeper understanding of the methodology.

•   *Handbook of autoethnography*, S. Holman Jones, T. Adams & C. Ellis (eds) (2016). This extensive handbook features an incredible richness of authorship divided into four sections – each with an introduction and several exemplar chapters. Although a little overwhelming at first, the text provides depth and breadth including a wide variety of interpretations and works by many seminal authors in the field.

- *Collaborative autoethnography*, H. Chang, F. Ngunjiri, Wambura & K.C. Hernandez (2013). Of particular interest for those looking to work with others, this book includes a wealth of information. Beginning with defining collaborative autoethnography, the text proceeds to identify different types within the method, reviews preparation for research teams, provides an overview of data collection and analysis, shares writing ideas and concludes with clear applications for the work.

- *Autoethnography as method*, H. Chang (2008). Perhaps a simpler read than the 'Handbook' above, Chang's text provides an excellent overview and analysis of the method. The organisation is particularly helpful as the 10 chapters are organised into three sections: conceptual framework, collecting autoethnographic data, and turning data into autoethnography.

- *International Congress of Qualitative Inquiry* (ICQI, http://icqi.org). At the time of writing this text, the ICGI will be entering its fourteenth iteration. The Congress features autoethnography as a special interest group and provides opportunities both to present within the methodology and learn from leaders in collaborative workshops.

References

Adams, T., Holman Jones, S., & Ellis, C. (2015). *Autoethnography: Understanding qualitative research*. New York: Oxford University Press.

Ai, B. (2016). Experiencing different identity prototypes in learning and teaching English: A Chinese learner's autoethnography. *Changing English, 23*(3), 280–291.

Behar, R. (1998). A sixth memo for the millennium: Vulnerability. Retrieved 10 August 2012 from www.mit.edu/bhdavis/BeharLec.html.

Bolen, D.M. (2012). Toward an applied communication relational inqueery: Autoethnography, co-constructed narrative, and relational futures. Unpublished doctoral dissertation, Wayne State University.

Brooks, C., & Dinan Thompson, M. (2015). Insideness and outsideness: An autoethnography of a primary physical education specialist teacher. *European Physical Education Review, 21*(3), 325–339.

Cameron, E. (2012). De/reconstructing my athlete–student–teacher self: A critical autoethnography of resistance in physical education teacher education (PETE). *PHEnex Journal, 4*(2), 1–9.

Carless, D. (2012). Negotiating sexuality and masculinity in school sport: An autoethnography. *Sport, Education and Society, 17*(5), 607–625.

Cassidy, T., Kidman, L., & Dudfield, O. (2015). Insights in to the process of creating a coach development programme: The opportunities and challenges of ethnodrama. *Qualitative Research in Sport, Exercise and Health, 7*(5), 589–605.

Chang, H. (2008). *Autoethnography as method*. Walnut Creek, CA: Left Coast Press.

Chang, H., Ngunjiri, F. Wambura, & Hernandez, K.C. (2013). *Collaborative autoethnography*. Walnut Creek, CA: Left Coast Press.

Denzin, N., & Lincoln, Y. (2011). Introduction: The discipline and practice of qualitative research. In N. Denzin & Y. Lincoln (eds). *The SAGE handbook of qualitative research* (4th ed., pp. 1–20). Thousand Oaks, CA: Sage.

Ellis, C. (1993). 'There are survivors': Telling a story of sudden death. *The Sociological Quarterly, 34,* 711–730.

Ellis, C. (2004). *The ethnographic I: A methodological novel about autoethnography.* Walnut Creek, CA: AltaMira Press.

Ellis, C., & Bochner, A.P. (eds). (1996). Special issue: Taking ethnography into the twenty-first century. *Journal of Contemporary Ethnography, 25*(1).

Ellis, C., & Bochner, A.P. (2000). Autoethnography, personal narrative, reflexivity. In N.K. Denzin & Y.S. Lincoln (eds). *Handbook of qualitative research* (2nd edition, pp.733–768). Thousand Oaks, CA: Sage.

Ellis, C., Adams, E., & Bochner, A. (2011). Autoethnography: An overview. *Historical Social Research, 36*(4), 273–290.

Farrell, L., Bourgeois-Law, G., Regehr, G., & Ajjawi, R. (2015). Autoethnography: Introducing 'I' into medical education research. *Medical Education Research, 49*(10), 974–982.

Fisette, J.L. (2013). The stigmatised physical educator. *Qualitative Research in Sport, Exercise and Health, 7*(4), 466–487.

Foley, S., Valenzuela, A., Denzin, N.K., & Lincoln, Y.S. (2005). *The SAGE handbook of Qualitative research* (3rd edition). Los Angeles, CA: Sage.

Geertz, C. (1975). On the nature of anthropological understanding: Not extraordinary empathy but readily observable symbolic forms enable the anthropologist to grasp the unarticulated concepts that inform the lives and cultures of other peoples. *American Scientist, 63*(1), 47–53.

Geist-Martin, P., Gates, L., Wiering, L., Kirby, E., Houston, R., Lilly, A., & Moreno, J. (2010). Exemplifying collaborative autoethnographic practice via shared stories of mothering. *Journal of Research Practice, 6*(1), 8.

Hamdan, A. (2012). Autoethnography as a genre of qualitative research: A journey inside out. *International Journal of Qualitative Methods, 11*(5), 585–606.

Hernandez, K.C., Wambura Ngunjiri, F., & Chang, H. (2015). Exploiting the margins in higher education: A collaborative autoethnography of three foreign-born female faculty of color. *International Journal of Qualitative Studies in Education, 28*(5), 533–551.

Holman Jones, S., Adams, T., & Ellis, C. (eds). (2016). *Handbook of autoethnography.* New York: Routledge.

Holmes, K. (2015). Reflections on teaching and learning in undergraduate education: An auto-ethnographical reflection on storytelling as a portal to mindfulness. *Creative Approaches to Research, 8*(1), 86–99.

Holt, N.L. (2003). Representation, legitimation, and autoethnography: An autoethnographic writing story. *International Journal of Qualitative Methods, 2*(1), 18–28.

Kalmbach Phillips, D., Harris, G., Legard Larson, M., & Higgins, K. (2009). Trying on – being in – becoming: Four women's journey(s) in feminist post-structural theory. *Qualitative Inquiry, 15*(9), 1455–1479.

Kretchmar, S. (2008). The increasing utility of elementary school physical education: A mixed blessing and unique challenge. *The Elementary School Journal, 108*(3), 161–170.

Legge, M. (2014). Autoethnography and teacher education: Snapshot stories of cultural encounter. *Australian Journal of Teacher Education, 39*(5), 117–134.

Malinowski, B. (1989). *A diary in the strict sense of the term.* Stanford, CA: Stanford University Press.

McParland, S. (2013). The gender game: Rewriting the rules of basketball through autoethnography. *Sport History Review, 44,* 25–37.

Mills, J.P. (2015). An (AUTO)ethnographic account of constructing, deconstructing, and partially reconstructing a coaching identity. *Qualitative Research in Sport, 7*(5), 606–619.

Morimoto, L. (2008). Teaching as transgression: The autoethnography of a fat physical education instructor. *Proteus, 25*(2), 29–36.

Newbold, G., Ross, J. I., Jones, R. S., Richards, S. C., & Lenza, M. (2014). Prison research from the inside. *Qualitative Inquiry, 20*(4), 439–448.

Purdy, L., Potrac, P., & Jones, R. (2008). Power, consent and resistance: an autoethnography of competitive rowing. *Sport, Education and Society, 13*(3), 319–336.

Sparkes, A. C. (2002). *Telling tales in sport and physical activity.* Champaign, IL: Human Kinetics.

Sparkes, A. C., Brown, D. H. K., & Partington, E. (2007). Bodies as bearers of value: The transmission of jock culture via the 'Twelve Commandments'. *Sport, Education and Society, 12*(3), 295–316.

Sparkes, A. C., Brown, D. H. K., & Partington, E. (2010). The 'jock body' and the social construction of space: The performance and positioning of cultural identity. *Space and Culture, 13*(3), 333–347.

Taylor, M., Klein, E. J., & Abrams, L. (2014). Tensions of reimagining our roles as teacher educators in a third space: Revisiting a co/autoethnography through a faculty lens. *Studying Teacher Education, 10*(1), 3–19.

Vone'che, J. (2001). Identity and narrative in Piaget's autobiographies. In J. Brockmeier & D. Carbaugh (eds). *Narrative and identity: Studies in autoethnography, self, and culture* (pp. 219–246). Amsterdam, Netherlands: John Benjamins.

Wakeman, S. (2014). Fieldwork, biography and emotion: Doing criminological autoethnography. *British Journal of Criminology, 54*(5), 705–721.

Wall, S. (2006). An autoethnography on learning about autoethnography, *International Journal of Qualitative Methods, 5*(2), 2–12.

Wall, S. (2008). Easier said than done: Writing an autoethnography. *International Journal of Qualitative Methods, 7*(1), 38–53.

5

SELF-STUDY OF PRACTICE

Introduction

Self-study of practice researchers examine the intertwined nature of self and practice by closely considering the self-*in*-practice (Ovens & Fletcher, 2014a), requiring a strong focus on the role of one's personal and professional identities. This focus on the self-in-practice helps distinguish it from autoethnography (a focus on the self in culture) and action research (a focus on practice). Some consider self-study a moral imperative for practitioners who are invested in deepening their understanding of practice (Pinnegar & Hamilton, 2009). In this chapter, the strengths and challenges of self-study of practice are described, leading to a discussion of established criteria deemed to indicate quality in self-study research (LaBoskey, 2004). Building upon Brown's (2011) call for those in the fields of physical education, youth sport and health to engage in self-study as a form of professional learning, several examples will be reviewed and the unique insights afforded by self-study explained.

What is self-study of practice?

Most people who are familiar with self-study of practice would describe it in its simplest terms as a qualitative research methodology (Pinnegar & Hamilton, 2009). In addition, it might be identified as a form of practitioner research that has had particular resonance with teacher educators – those practitioners who teach teachers (Vanassche & Kelchtermans, 2015). It has also been employed by classroom teachers who study their practice (Attard & Armour, 2005), as well as by other professionals, such as coaches (Bowles, 2016). The significance of self-study of practice research to teacher educators is evident in one of the more common variations of its name: self-study of teacher education practice research (S-STEP). The S-STEP acronym serves two overlapping purposes: it attaches a certain type of practice to self-study research (teacher education practice, hence the TEP in the acronym) while also distancing it from more generic forms of self-study. For example, self-study has been a term used to describe research conducted by institutions into their processes, much like programme reviews or evaluations. According to Loughran (2004), the purpose of studying the self when the self is framed as an institution is to question its structures and functions or to find ways the institution might function more effectively. The main feature that distinguishes self-study of practice research (including S-STEP) from earlier programmatic forms of self-study research is that S-STEP acknowledges and gives voice to the individuals engaged in researching their practice, while the earlier versions define the self in an institutional sense without specific attention paid to the individual selves who work in the institution. For the purposes of this book, we focus on self-study of practice research and not institutional forms of self-study.

What are the main features of self-study of practice?

Self-study of practice draws from a variety of qualitative traditions, including those described elsewhere in this book. In the same way that the S-STEP research movement has given voice to individual teacher educators who are engaged in the practices they are researching, self-study of practice similarly gives voice to individual practitioners but on a broader scale – including, for the purposes of this book, teacher educators, coach educators, teachers, coaches, recreation leaders, sport providers and other practitioners in the field. Self-study of practice researchers are committed to their ongoing professional learning and explore their assumptions, beliefs and actions as they are enacted in practice.

The features of self-study require researchers to interrogate their assumptions and open up new interpretations and possibilities for practice. However, this can be quite challenging as it is difficult to change things that inform one's sense of self. Yet, as Loughran (2004) suggests, unless a self-study researcher makes him- or herself vulnerable through exposing their doubts, confusions, failures and uncertainties, this type of research is at risk of becoming a mechanism for self-justification (or navel gazing) and subsequently loses its potential for transformation. Vanassche and Kelchtermans (2015) offer a helpful summary of the purpose of self-study of practice research, suggesting it has 'always been to move beyond the particularities of practice by making public the developed understanding . . . in order to make them informative for others and available for critical debate' (ibid., p. 509).

The field of self-study of practice has expanded quite rapidly over the last twenty years suggesting it resonates with the intentions and aspirations of many practitioner researchers. Despite its broad appeal, like narrative inquiry there is a lack of consensus around what defines self-study of practice research. This might be because self-study of practice research tends to reflect a clear *focus* rather than a clear *set of methods* (Loughran, 2004). Ovens and Fletcher (2014a) offered one definition, outlining three common characteristics – community, stance and desire – that self-study of practice researchers share and which enable their work to be identified as self-study.

1   *Community*. Self-study of practice researchers are part of a professional community of practitioners who inquire into their own professional practice. By being members of this professional community, self-study of practice researchers are committed to sharing their work so it may be critiqued to enable rich and meaningful conversations about the processes and people involved in teaching and learning. For practitioners who are members of universities or colleges or other institutions where there may be a formal requirement to conduct research, such work might be shared at conferences or in journals or books. For practitioners who do not have these responsibilities, their self-study research might be shared among colleagues in or across schools, clubs or other types of professional learning communities.

2   *Stance*. Self-study of practice researchers take an inquiry-oriented stance towards researching how they think, know and act in the specific sociocultural and geopolitical contexts in which they conduct their practice. Self-study of practice researchers are practitioners who acknowledge that the learners, schools, sports clubs and places of their work are unique. As such, it is possible that some broad understandings of practice generated by others can be applied to one's own practice (for example, some principles of effective instruction); however, there is a clear understanding that what works for someone, somewhere, at some point in time might not necessarily work for other practitioners, in other schools or clubs, with other learners. Practitioners must therefore constantly ask questions of themselves, their learners and their contexts. There is also an acknowledgement that practice is incredibly complex, and an inquiring attitude provides the curiosity to continue questioning what works, what doesn't, when, where, why and with whom.

3   *Desire*. By framing the inquiry simultaneously on the self *and* practice, the practitioner expresses a desire to be more, to improve, to learn and to better understand. The inner drive self-study of practice researchers have towards improvement can often lead to personal and/or professional transformation.

It may seem from the characteristics described that self-study of practice research is simply a group of people who have a shared desire to inquire and improve. However, there is more to it. In the next section we identify several features of self-study of practice research design that serve as guidelines for quality and allow the work to be described as such.

LaBoskey's (2004) guidelines for self-study research design

While several authors have offered suggestions about what constitutes strong self-study of practice research design (Bullough & Pinnegar, 2001; Samaras, 2010), LaBoskey's chapter in the *International Handbook of Self-study of Teaching and Teacher Education Practice* (Loughran, Hamilton, LaBoskey & Russell, 2004) represents a robust set of suggestions to guide self-study of practice research designs. She offered the following ideas.

Self-study of practice research is self-initiated and self-focused

The practitioner and not an external group or body (such as a school district or sporting organisation) selects the issues, challenges and problems of professional practice. Moreover, there is a considered focus on the ways a practitioner's assumptions, beliefs, values and identities shape and are influenced by practice.

Self-study of practice research is aimed towards improvement

The improvement being aimed for is not necessarily effectiveness or 'best practice'; more often the improvement sought is in terms of understanding one's self, one's practice, one's context or the students with whom one is working. Self-study is therefore future-oriented and begins with a research question (which can be very general or very specific) to shape an inquiry into practice.

Self-study of practice research is interactive

This guideline may confuse those new to self-study; after all, doesn't a focus on the self suggest a lone enterprise? It can; however, gathering multiple perspectives of practice allows us to 'challenge our assumptions and biases, reveal our inconsistencies, [and] expand our potential interpretations' (LaBoskey, 2004, p. 849). Common sources of interaction for a practitioner researcher include:

- Colleagues who, as critical friends, might observe and provide feedback on a lesson or practice session, or engage in a caring but challenging discussion about a situation or set of circumstances. This can be a one-off or ongoing source of interaction beneficial to all involved.
- Students or other learners who might be asked for their perspectives on one's practice (through conversation or written feedback).

Self-study of practice researchers draw from multiple, primarily qualitative, methods and data sources

Sources a self-study of practice researcher might generate throughout an inquiry include lesson or session plans, reflective diaries or journal entries, observation notes from a colleague, a recorded discussion with a critical friend, student/learner work samples or forms of student/learner feedback about teaching. The main focus of these data sources should be on the particular issue or problem of practice the self-study researcher has identified at the outset of the inquiry.

'Validation' of self-study of practice research is based on trustworthiness

For those conducting research to be shared at academic conferences or in peer-reviewed journals, features that make the research credible, authentic and trustworthy are crucial to helping determine a study's merit. These considerations might not be as important for practitioners conducting research to be shared with colleagues in a department or club, but they are still worth considering. Self-study research is deemed trustworthy when other members of the community in which the work is being shared become involved and can benefit from it (LaBoskey, 2004). To allow others into the research process requires self-study of practice researchers to:

- be clear about the issues of practice being explored;
- provide rich descriptive details about the context in which the work is taking place;
- make themselves vulnerable by exposing uncertainties, contradictions, and shortcomings in one's practice;
- create an audit trail of the data analysed to arrive at the insights gained; and
- invite others to ask themselves about the extent to which the interpretations make sense to them given their own understandings of practice.

Self-study of practice researchers do not necessarily seek answers to their problems; rather, knowledge of the self and of practice is reframed and an understanding about the complexities of professional practice is revealed. Importantly, these insights are partial and temporary, and the acknowledgement of the fleeting nature of understanding provides motivation for the researcher to continue inquiring into practice.

A key summative point about conducting self-study of practice research lies in the nature of reporting the outcomes of the inquiry with others. Taking an inquiry stance requires self-study of practice researchers to go beyond the stories of practice. Their task is to identify, generate, articulate and share what knowledge about practice has been derived as a result of conducting an inquiry to make a difference beyond the individual conducting the research (Loughran, 2010).

A brief history of self-study of practice

In the early 1990s several teacher educators met to discuss many of the issues and challenges they were facing in their practice. At that time, the broader educational research community was quite happy for teacher educators to be researched by others who were removed from the daily routines of teacher education but who also were not sensitive to the messiness and complexities faced by practitioners in teacher education contexts. Among the main things shared at these initial meetings was a frustration that there was not a sophisticated or sufficient research methodology that allowed teacher educators to use their intimate knowledge of their contexts, programmes, students and practices to contribute to and build knowledge in teacher education research. In his vice-presidential speech to the American Educational Research Association in 1999, noted teacher education researcher Kenneth Zeichner said 'the self-study in teacher education movement . . . [to that time] has probably been the most significant development ever in the field of teacher education research' (Zeichner, 1999, p. 8).

Since the early 1990s, the S-STEP network has grown to include an international group of teacher educators who study their practice and there has been a steady growth in interest from practitioners in physical education and related fields. For example, two edited collections of self-study of practice research in physical education (Ovens & Fletcher, 2014b; 2015) contain a diverse, international collection of studies, exploring topics such as: learning new forms of practice, the complexities of peer teaching, unpacking the process of pedagogical innovations, outdoor education, racism and social justice, and self-study as professional learning. These works have provided some insights into how practitioner researchers understand and inquire into the problems of practice inherent in physical education and youth sport.

How self-study of practice has been used in professional settings

Vanassche and Kelchtermans (2015) conducted a thorough review of self-study of practice research to identify some of the main outcomes. Their review focused only on self-studies conducted by teacher educators working in higher education institutions and so it is limited in terms of what it tells us about how self-study of practice has contributed to knowledge and understanding in other professional settings. By looking at self-studies published between 1990 and 2015, they identified some of the following main strands of self-study research:

- The influence of a practitioner's biography on their identities and practices (Bullock & Ritter, 2011). Many times these self-studies have been conducted in times of transition – for example, in the shift from classroom teacher to university teacher educator (Dinkelman, Margolis & Sikkenga, 2006).
- Inquiries into the nature and impact of various interventions or innovations in teacher education courses or programmes (Brandenburg, 2008). For example, some have focused on attempts to enact pedagogies that promote social justice or critical pedagogy (Ragoonaden, 2015), while others have looked at specific aspects of the practicum (Bullock, 2012).
- Analyses of the differences between practitioners' beliefs, intentions, and actions in teaching (Berry, 2007). For example, 'does what I believe and value in teaching align with how I actually teach?'
- The description and enactment of particular theories or philosophies of practice. For example, practices that reflect social constructivist approaches to learning, ways to highlight or examine embodied emotions in teaching (Forgasz, McDonough & Berry, 2014) or feminist pedagogies (Coia & Taylor, 2013).
- The ways in which collaborative self-study (i.e. conducted with critical friends or in professional learning communities) has enabled new insights into or understandings of the self-in-practice (Kitchen, Ciuffetelli Parker & Gallagher, 2008; Schuck & Russell, 2005).

Although there is diversity in how the researchers approached their work, a closer look reveals fairly tight alignment with the suggestions for quality in self-study research design (such as those offered by LaBoskey, 2004). That is, all the work is self-initiated or self-focused; it is aimed towards improvement, typically in terms of improved understanding; it involves interaction between several participants or texts; it draws from multiple data sources; and, by sharing the work, the researchers are implicitly asking readers to judge the trustworthiness of the research by considering the extent to which the interpretations and insights ring true for readers based on their experiences and local contexts.

How self-study has been used in physical education and youth sport

Although self-study of practice research has been used since the mid-1990s, it has taken quite a long time to see its influence in physical education and youth sport. Prior to the mid-2000s, examples of self-study in physical education and youth sport settings tended to reflect institutional evaluations, where the self was framed as an institution (e.g. a specific programme) rather than an individual. The work of Metzler and colleagues at Georgia State University (GSU) (Metzler & Blankenship, 2000, 2008) represents this type of approach. Their work offered a deep and rigorous examination of the PETE programme at GSU, considering the overall programme foci, the outcomes of teacher candidates, and the ways in which the many layers of their teacher education programme were assessed. While this type of self-study research is valuable and makes important contributions to the literature, it is distinct from the approach to self-study of practice taken in this book where the inquiry gives voice to the individuals working with learners and who have an intimate knowledge of the practices they are engaged in.

Most self-study of practice research conducted in physical education and youth sport has involved teacher educators based in universities who have examined their identities and practices as they teach teachers. Prior to the two edited collections on self-study of practice in PETE (Ovens & Fletcher, 2014b, 2015) there were few examples in the physical education and youth sport literature. Physical education teacher educators conducted some of that research (Hopper & Sandford, 2004); however, the focus was on teacher education in a broad sense rather than on PETE. This is not to identify this focus as a limitation but the large target audience for that work meant that many of its main points did not reach physical education teacher educators. That began to shift following the publication of MacPhail's (2011) research, where she outlined her beliefs about professional learning and offered some examples of how she models lifelong learning for the future teachers she works with. Since this time, there has been a steady growth in the amount and types of self-study of practice research conducted in physical education and youth sport.

Research in physical education and youth sport that has used self-study of practice methodology can be thematised in a similar way to that done by Vanassche and Kelchtermans (2015). For example, physical education teacher educators have considered the ways in which their identities, theories and practices intersect. Tannehill (2016) shared her metaphor for teaching (a salmon swimming upriver) and how that represented her learning and practice over her extensive career as a physical education teacher educator. In a similar way, Tim articulated several principles that guided his PETE practice based on social constructivist theories of learning, providing evidence of how he enacted those principles and his students' experiences of their learning (Fletcher, 2016). Ash and Tim examined the challenges they faced in making transitions from physical education teachers to teacher educators, noting difficulties in adapting practices perceived as being successful in schools to practices that are appropriate for pre-service teachers' learning (Casey & Fletcher, 2012). Similarly, Richards and Ressler (2016) showed how self-study was able to help a new faculty member who did not have previous school teaching experience examine his assumptions and beliefs about teaching teachers, and navigate the diverse and sometimes competing roles in a new teaching position at a university.

There are also several examples that consider interventions or innovations in PETE courses or programmes. For instance, Ovens (2014) explored the problematic nature of peer teaching in teacher education, exposing the often unseen power dynamics among students within a class. Ní Chróinín, Fletcher and O'Sullivan (2015) examined the processes involved in teaching teachers how to promote meaningful experiences in physical education. Another pedagogical innovation that has been examined has been the challenges of teaching through a models-based approach in PETE (Fletcher & Casey, 2014). This study revealed a need for teacher educators to reframe parts of their school-based practices while also being willing to learn new practices they may not have employed if and when they were a school teacher. In a new development, Bowles (2016) used self-study of practice research to examine the challenges of implementing a game sense approach into his coaching of a women's Gaelic football team. Such research shows the promise of self-study of practice for coaches, coach educators and other professionals in physical education and sport-related fields.

Some authors have analysed the challenges in aligning their beliefs and actions in PETE. For example, Bruce (2013), Cameron (2014), and Flory and Walton-Fisette (2015) examined the ways they enact pedagogies that promote social justice and critical pedagogies, noting students' openness and resistance to such approaches, and the difficulties faced in translating personal beliefs into practices. North (2016) described his assumptions about teaching an outdoor education course and the ways students' responses and learning in that course conflicted with his interpretations of their experience. Consequently, this led him to reconsider his approaches and acknowledge the importance of his students' perspectives in considering his pedagogy of teacher education.

Collaborative self-studies have also been employed in PETE research. For example, Tannehill, Parker, Tindall, Moody, and MacPhail (2015) used collaborative self-study to identify and create a shared vision for the PETE programme at the University of Limerick in Ireland. This represents a new wave of self-study of practice research in PETE, as most to this point has been confined to one or two individuals working in a programme rather than that of a collective or team.

Although teacher or coach educators working in higher education institutions have conducted the bulk of self-study of practice research, there are several examples of self-studies conducted by teachers working in schools or school districts. Karl Attard (Attard, 2008; Attard & Armour, 2005, 2006) conducted his self-study research while working as a physical education teacher and graduate student in Malta. A main focus of his research was being attentive to the challenges of implementing a new syllabus while engaging in collaborative professional learning with colleagues (Attard & Armour, 2005). In a summary of his self-study research, Attard explains: 'through experiencing self-study, I have come to believe that the most important aspect of teacher learning is the examination of one's own tacit understandings and taken-for-granted assumptions' (Attard, 2014, p. 31). This statement captures the essence of self-study of practice research – that one must necessarily consider the intertwined influence of one's self and one's practice.

Ash also published self-study research on his practices as a physical education teacher (Casey, 2012). In that particular research project, he looked at the ways self-study enabled him to attend to pedagogical and curricular change in his practice – something that was self-driven but that he came to acknowledge was influenced by 'extra-individual' conditions, such as students, colleagues and institutions.

Both Attard's and Casey's work show the hybridity of self-study research – or what might be described as principled pragmatism. At various times each author identified his work as autoethnographic (Attard & Armour, 2005), critical reflection (Attard & Armour, 2006) or insider-action research (Casey, 2012), revealing how hard it can be to 'pin down' definitions of practitioner research genres, and, in particular, self-study. However, a quick glance over Ovens and Fletcher's (2014a) suggestions or LaBoskey's (2004) guidelines shows some alignment with the characteristics of self-study of practice research and the research conducted by Attard and Casey, respectively. Perhaps this also suggests that it may not be the mode of inquiry used that is most important – it is the commitment to systematically and critically examining one's identities and practice that is crucial if a practitioner seeks to better understand her or his own practice and thus more strongly and positively influence student learning.

The possibilities of self-study research in physical education and youth sport

All examples of self-study of practice research – both in physical education/youth sport and in educational research more broadly – demonstrate a commitment to share the insights gained from the work to spark debate among the relevant communities of practitioners whom the work is addressed to, thus enabling others to learn from it. As members of the physical education community, we have learned a great deal through reading the research conducted by these practitioners, and some of us have been able to apply some of their insights and understandings to how we think about and go about teaching physical education teachers. This says a great deal about the ways in which the practitioner researchers involved have provided rich descriptions of the contexts in which they work, and outlined the beliefs and assumptions brought to their inquiries. Moreover, it highlights the power of self-study of practice research in being able to reach beyond the individuals who conduct the research to generate important and insightful understanding of knowledge about professional practice.

In taking a future-oriented perspective on the potential of self-study of practice research for physical education, both O'Sullivan (2014) and Tinning (2014) herald the ways in which self-study offers practitioner researchers an opportunity to share their insights and understandings about teaching and learning with others in a 'discourse community' (a group of professionals who share similar dispositions). While many educational authorities use the term 'reflective practitioner' as an indicator of professional competence, there can be a tendency to frame reflective practice as one of many technical skills on a checklist. However, use of the term 'reflective practitioner' has become so ubiquitous to become almost a buzzword, with little meaning attached to what it might constitute. Tinning (2014) views the development of a community who share self-study research as a way to go beyond the technical, enabling practitioner researchers to embed their autobiographies in theorising their practice.

So what? Why does this community building and theorising matter? It matters because pedagogy is a reflection of social and cultural practices, and understanding how practitioners locate themselves socially and culturally will necessarily inform how they approach their work and engage with learners. The commitment to sharing self-study of practice research then allows the knowledge generated by individual practitioner researchers to be critiqued and debated by others. This, in turn, leads to more rigorous and nuanced understandings of the complexity of professional practice in the contexts in which those practices occur.

Self-study of practice research provides inquiry-oriented practitioners with a framework to conduct action-oriented, forward-thinking research. The area of inquiry is not pre-determined by an overseeing authority (such as a principal); rather, based on their intimate knowledge of the learners and contexts in which they work, it is the practitioner who decides the topics to pursue. Importantly, the focus of self-study of practice should not be to provide some self-justification for a practitioner's practice but to be self-critical, honest, open, vulnerable and transparent in order to shine light on and deepen understanding about valuable, troublesome, problematic or complex aspects of practice. For teachers and coaches, there are many opportunities to conduct research on their respective selves-in-practice and it should involve the input of others – such as learners, colleagues and texts. The outcomes of the inquiry can be shared formally or informally with colleagues (in a club, school, district, or professional organisation), with the aim being to build a shared knowledge of practice and to pose further questions to pursue in the future.

Further reading and resources

Books and journals

Loughran, J. (2010). Seeking knowledge for teaching: Moving beyond stories. *Studying Teacher Education, 6*(3), 221–226. Contains important suggestions to help self-study researchers consider how their work can help others learn.

Ovens, A. & Fletcher, T. (eds). (2014). *Self-study of physical education teacher education: The interplay of practice and scholarship.* Dordrecht: Springer. The first edited collection of self-study research in physical education.

Ovens, A. & Fletcher, T. (eds). (2015). Special issue: Self-study in health, sport, and physical education. *Asia-Pacific Journal of Health, Sport, and Physical Education, 6*(3). The second edited collection of self-study research in physical education.

Samaras, A.P. (2010). *Self-study teacher research: Improving your practice through collaborative inquiry.* Thousand Oaks, CA: Sage Publications. An excellent resource aimed towards practitioners who are interested in using self-study of practice research to improve their practice.

Other

Studying Teacher Education. This is an academic journal that publishes self-study of practice research several times a year. For those who are not members of an institution that subscribes, there is a cost for individual subscriptions or for accessing individual articles. See www.tandfonline.com/toc/cste20/current.

The International Conference on Self-study of Teacher Education Practice or 'Castle Conference'. This conference is held bi-annually at Herstmonceux Castle in the United Kingdom. Self-study researchers present their work (mainly teacher educators but other practitioners have presented and are welcome to attend or present) to others in the self-study community. On the website, you can access and download the proceedings from previous Castle Conferences for free. See www.castleconfer ence.com/conference-history.html.

References

Attard, K. (2008). Uncertainty for the reflective practitioner: A blessing in disguise. *Reflective Practice, 9*(3), 307–317.

Attard, K. (2014). Self-study as professional development: Some reflections from experience. In A. Ovens & T. Fletcher (eds), *Self-study in physical education teacher education* (pp. 29–43). Dordrecht: Springer.

Attard, K., & Armour, K.M. (2005). Learning to become a learning professional: Reflections on one year of teaching. *European Journal of Teacher Education, 28*(2), 195–207.

Attard, K., & Armour, K.M. (2006). Reflecting on reflection: A case study of one teacher's early-career professional learning. *Physical Education and Sport Pedagogy, 11*(3), 209–229.

Berry, A. (2007). Reconceptualizing teacher educator knowledge as tensions: Exploring the tension between valuing and reconstructing experience. *Studying Teacher Education, 3*(2), 117–134.

Bowles, R. (2016). 'Two steps forward, one step back': A coaching self-study examining the use of game sense during a Gaelic football season. Paper presented at the AIESEP International Conference, Laramie WY, 8–11 June.

Brandenburg, R.T. (2008). *Powerful pedagogy: Self-study of a teacher educator's practice.* Dordrecht: Springer.

Brown, T.D. (2011). More than glimpses in the mirror: An argument for self-study in the professional learning of physical education teachers. *Asia-Pacific Journal of Health, Sport and Physical Education, 2*(1), 19–32.

Bruce, J. (2013). Dancing on the edge: A self-study exploring postcritical possibilities in physical education. *Sport, Education and Society, 18*(6), 807–824.

Bullock, S.M. (2012). Creating a space for the development of professional knowledge: A self-study of supervising teacher candidates during practicum placements. *Studying Teacher Education, 8*(2), 143–156.

Bullock, S.M., & Ritter, J.K. (2011). Exploring the transition into academia through collaborative self-study. *Studying Teacher Education, 7*, 171–181.

Bullough, R.V. Jr., and Pinnegar, S. (2001). Guidelines for quality in autobiographical forms of self-study research. *Educational Researcher, 30*(3), 13–21.

Cameron, E. (2014). A journey of critical scholarship in physical education teacher education. In A. Ovens & T. Fletcher (eds), *Self-study in physical education teacher education* (pp. 99–115). Dordrecht: Springer.

Casey, A. (2012). A self-study using action research: Changing site expectations and practice stereotypes. *Educational Action Research, 20*(2), 219–232.

Casey, A., & Fletcher, T. (2012). Trading places: From physical education teachers to teacher educators. *Journal of Teaching in Physical Education, 31*(4), 362–380.

Coia, L., & Taylor, M. (2013). Uncovering our feminist pedagogy: A co/autoethnography. *Studying Teacher Education, 9*(1), 3–17.

Dinkelman, T., Margolis, J., & Sikkenga, K. (2006). From teacher to teacher educator: Experiences, expectations, and expatriation. *Studying Teacher Education, 2*(1), 5–23.

Fletcher, T. (2016). Developing principles of physical education teacher education practice through self-study. *Physical Education and Sport Pedagogy, 21*(4), 347–365.

Fletcher, T., & Casey, A. (2014). The challenges of models-based practice in physical education teacher education: A collaborative self-study. *Journal of Teaching in Physical Education, 33*(3), 403–421.

Flory, S.B., & Walton-Fisette, J.L. (2015). Teaching sociocultural issues to pre-service physical education teachers: A self-study. *Asia-Pacific Journal of Health, Sport and Physical Education, 6*(3), 245–257.

Forgasz, R., McDonough, S., & Berry, A. (2014). Embodied approaches to S-STEP research into teacher educator emotion. In D. Garbett & A. Ovens (eds), *Proceedings of the Tenth International Conference on Self-study of Teacher Education Practice* (pp. 82–84). Auckland: University of Auckland Press.

Hopper, T., & Sanford, K. (2004). Representing multiple perspectives of self-as-teacher: School-integrated teacher education and self-study. *Teacher Education Quarterly, 31*(2), 57–74.

Kitchen, J., Ciuffetelli Parker, D., & Gallagher, T. (2008). Authentic conversation as faculty development: Establishing a self-study group in a faculty of education. *Studying Teacher Education, 4*(2), 157–171.

LaBoskey, V.K. (2004). The methodology of teaching and its theoretical underpinnings. In J.J. Loughran, M.L. Hamilton, V.K. LaBoskey, & T. Russell (eds), *International handbook of self-study of teaching and teacher education practices* (pp. 817–869). Dordrecht: Kluwer Academic Press.

Loughran, J.J. (2004). A history and context of self-study of teaching and teacher education practices. In J. Loughran, M.L. Hamilton, V.K. LaBoskey, & T. Russell (eds), *International handbook of self-study of teaching and teacher education practices* (pp. 7–40). Dordrecht: Kluwer Academic Press.

Loughran, J. (2010). Seeking knowledge for teaching teaching: Moving beyond stories. *Studying Teacher Education, 6*(3), 221–226.

Loughran, J.J., Hamilton, M.L., LaBoskey, V.K., & Russell, T. (eds). (2004). *International handbook of self-study of teaching and teacher education practices.* Dordrecht: Kluwer Academic Press.

MacPhail, A. (2011). Professional learning as a physical education teacher educator. *Physical Education & Sport Pedagogy, 16*(4), 435–451.

Metzler, M.W., & Blankenship, B.T. (2000). Teacher education program assessment and the GSU PETE assessment project. *Journal of Teaching in Physical Education, 19*(4), 395–401.

Metzler, M.W., & Blankenship, B.T. (2008). Taking the next step: Connecting teacher education, research on teaching, and programme assessment. *Teaching and Teacher Education, 24*(4), 1098–1111.

Ní Chróinín, D., Fletcher, T., & O'Sullivan, M. (2015). Using self-study to explore the processes of pedagogical innovation in physical education teacher education. *Asia-Pacific Journal of Health, Sport and Physical Education, 6*(3), 273–286.

North, C. (2016). Swinging between infatuation and disillusionment: Learning about teaching teachers through self-study. *Physical Education and Sport Pedagogy, 22*(4), 390–402.

O'Sullivan, M. (2014). Where we go from here: Developing pedagogies for PETE and the use of self-study in physical education and teacher education. In A. Ovens & T. Fletcher (eds), *Self-study in physical education teacher education* (pp. 169–180). Dordrecht: Springer.

Ovens, A. (2014). Disturbing practice in teacher education through peer-teaching. In A. Ovens & T. Fletcher (eds), *Self-study in physical education teacher education* (pp. 87–98). Dordrecht: Springer.

Ovens, A., & Fletcher, T. (2014a). Doing self-study: The art of turning inquiry on yourself. In A. Ovens & T. Fletcher (eds), *Self-study in physical education teacher education: Exploring the interplay of practice and scholarship* (pp. 3–14). Dordrecht: Springer.

Ovens, A., & Fletcher, T. (eds). (2014b). *Self-study in physical education teacher education: Exploring the interplay of practice and scholarship.* Dordrecht: Springer.

Ovens, A., & Fletcher, T. (eds). (2015). Special issue: Self-study in health, sport, and physical education. *Asia-Pacific Journal of Health, Sport and Physical Education, 6*(3), 215–311.

Pinnegar, S., & Hamilton, M.L. (2009). *Self-study of practice as a genre of qualitative research: Theory, methodology, and practice.* Dordrecht: Springer.

Ragoonaden, K. (2015). Self-study of teacher education practices and critical pedagogy: The fifth moment in a teacher educator's journey. *Studying Teacher Education, 11*(1), 81–95.

Richards, K.A.R., & Ressler, J.D. (2016). A collaborative approach to self-study research in physical education teacher education. *Journal of Teaching in Physical Education, 35*(3), 290–295.

Samaras, A.P. (2010). *Self-study teacher research: Improving your practice through collaborative inquiry.* Thousand Oaks, CA: Sage.

Schuck, S., & Russell, T. (2005). Self-study, critical friendship, and the complexities of teacher education. *Studying Teacher Education, 1*(2), 107–121.

Tannehill, D. (2016). My journey to become a teacher educator. *Physical Education and Sport Pedagogy, 21*(1), 105–120.

Tannehill, D., Parker, M., Tindall, D., Moody, B., & MacPhail, A. (2015). Looking across and within: Studying ourselves as teacher educators. *Asia-Pacific Journal of Health, Sport and Physical Education*, 6(3), 299–311.

Tinning, R. (2014). Reading self-study in/for physical education: Revisiting the zeitgeist of reflection. In A. Ovens & T. Fletcher (eds), *Self-study in physical education teacher education* (pp. 153–167). Dordrecht: Springer.

Vanassche, E., & Kelchtermans, G. (2015). The state of the art in self-study of teacher education practices: A systematic literature review. *Journal of Curriculum Studies*, 47(4), 508–528.

Zeichner, K.M. (1999). The new scholarship in teacher education. *Educational Researcher*, 28(9), 4–15.

PART III

The purpose of Part III is to provide the reader with an opportunity to experience (albeit second hand) each of the methodologies as they were used in actual studies. These chapters serve as examples of the sequence and process involved in using a particular form of practitioner research in an empirical research project. Each chapter takes the reader through the research process from start to finish. It is important to note that our intent in these chapters is not to disseminate the results of the respective research projects but to describe the *process* of conducting each practitioner inquiry. In some cases, you may well eventually see the results of these studies published in practitioner or academic journals but they are presented here as examples of real-world practitioner research studies.

To write the chapters in Part III, each of us worked with a practitioner researcher who had conducted research using one of the four methodologies outlined in the book. As with Part II, we each took responsibility for a chapter in the section based on our experience working with the respective methodologies. In Chapter 6, Jo Bailey used action research to explore the implementation of cooperative learning to teach her students in the affective domain. Ash worked with Jo to describe the sequence she took in conducting the action research project. In Chapter 7, Brian Lewis illustrates the process he went through as he used narrative inquiry to better understand the experiences of Indigenous youth in an after-school programme based on wellness. Chapter 8 contains Jodi Harding-Kuriger's use of autoethnography to explore herself as a teacher, mother, coach and athletic director within the culture of school sport. And in Chapter 9, Ciara Griffin describes how she used self-study of practice methodology to analyse how she enacted pedagogies that promoted meaningful experiences for primary physical education students in two Irish schools.

To encourage readers to put themselves in the shoes of the practitioner researchers whose work is being described, we invite consideration of the following questions as you read the chapters in this section:

- What is an issue or problem of practice that I would like to explore? What questions do I want to address?
- To help me explore the issues I am interested in, would it help to invite a colleague as a co-inquirer or critical friend? If so, what qualities and characteristics should they have? Should they be familiar or unfamiliar with the context in which I work? Who might make a shortlist?
- What types of data or documentation would provide evidence to help me address the issues and questions I am interested in? How can I use information from students in an ethical way?
- Which of the four methodologies appeals to me? Why might that be so? What resources do I have in place to assist with reflective practice in a particular methodology?

6

USING ACTION RESEARCH TO PROMOTE LEARNING IN THE AFFECTIVE DOMAIN

Jo Bailey and Ash Casey

Situating the research: Jo's story

I'm the product of a traditional physical education programme (i.e. sport-centric, teacher-directed, and focused on sporting seasons) and I loved it. I relished being part of a team, I loved competition and being active simply felt good. As a newly qualified teacher (NQT) I did what many NQTs do and taught in a manner that largely emulated my own experiences. My primary concerns were (a) delivering content and (b) being in control of my classes. These concerns outweighed the need to focus on creating positive and cohesive classroom cultures beyond my students' relationships with me. I certainly didn't intentionally try to create positive and cohesive classroom cultures between the students themselves.

I've been fortunate to teach in very different educational environments: a secondary school in England, a secondary school in Hong Kong, and the high school in the USA where I currently teach. While cultural and social differences are very evident between these schools and countries, the quest to create a learning environment that supports every student – and where every student feels supported by both the teacher and their peers – has been a constant journey. I've become increasingly aware that while my own physical education experiences were highly enjoyable, this wasn't the case for many of my peers. Conversations with friends, colleagues, parents and community members about their experiences suggests that physical education is a polarising experience for many. Those that felt valued and were highly skilled enjoyed physical education. Others who felt that they lacked skill experienced a lowering of both their self-worth and, ultimately, their enjoyment of physical education. Over my career I've increasingly noted that many students have a fixed mindset when it comes to physical education. In short, while many students believe they 'can', many equally believe they 'can't' when it comes to skills or physical abilities.

Recently, and as a result of these observations, my teaching has been driven by the need to effectively address the affective domain in physical education (what Bloom, 1956, described as feelings, values, appreciation, enthusiasms, motivations and attitudes). This desire to positively impact the affective domain is driven and sustained by my belief that learning in physical education, and subsequent independent engagement in physical activity, will be limited and/or compromised unless the learning environment supports, nurtures and values all students at all levels. It troubled me immensely that previously my students didn't know each other's names after spending 45 minutes a day, 5 days a week, for 18 weeks in a class together. The fault for that is mine. In action research terms (see Chapter 2, and Figure 2.2 in particular) this is my 'think' moment as I don't ever want this to be the case again. Subsequently, I began to explore and plan new ways to create an inclusive and student-centred learning environment where the focus was on supporting everyone as they navigated through their personal physical education journey.

I'd already adopted a student-centred approach to teaching by the time I was introduced to the cooperative learning model. I started using the cooperative learning structure Jigsaw with an outdoor and adventure class I taught. The primary goal was for students to develop cohesion and a sense of class community using backyard games (outdoor recreational games played in the backyard/garden of the house or community park) as a lens. Each student was responsible for learning a different backyard game and then teaching it to their home group. I believe it was successful. The main reason was because of the built-in positive interdependence and individual accountability (see Dyson & Casey, 2016 for a fuller explanation). For the first time, at least from my perspective, every student appeared to be fully involved and fully invested in class. This change spurred me on. I wanted to learn more about cooperative learning and see what other strategies I could implement to support the development of the affective domain in physical education. However, I wanted to do this in an informed manner, one that allowed me to focus on the needs and personal development of my students and build future pedagogical change and curriculum enhancement on *bona fide* results rather than whims and gut feelings. This is when I turned to Ash and our project started.

Background of the research problem/issue

Physical, cognitive, social and affective learning outcomes have been positioned as key learning outcomes of physical education (Casey & Goodyear, 2015; Fernandez-Rio et al., 2017). While all learning domains are important, the affective domain is often difficult to define (Casey, in press; Hellison, 1987), observing affective development is complex and difficult to track (Witt, 2015), and effective procedures and practices to support affective learning and development are less well-defined and evidence-informed (Bailey et al., 2009).

The desire to explicitly impact the affective development of Jo's students, combined with a concern that this would be a difficult and less-well travelled pedagogical road, served as the catalyst for this action research project. That, and Jo's interest in using cooperative learning, served as our starting/thinking point. It represents the identification of a general problem or idea. What follows is an exploration of, and a reporting on, three cycles of think, plan, act, evaluate and reflect that underpin this study.

Aims of the research

In 2016, Jo attended Dean Dudley's presentation at the SHAPE America Conference on a Health Optimizing Physical Education (HOPE) Assessment Framework (see Dudley, Goodyear, & Baxter, 2016). This framework outlined levels of student achievement for each of the cognitive, affective, social, psychomotor and physical activity domains. Student achievement in each domain was assessed using the following levels: 'Not Achieving', 'Attention Needed', 'Working Towards Outcomes', 'Achieving Outcomes' and 'Exceeding Outcomes'. The 'Achieving Outcomes' and 'Exceeding Outcomes' levels were separated by a progression threshold. Dudley et al. (2016) argue that if a student is at the progression threshold in one or more domains, attention should be shifted to the domains where the student is not reaching the threshold. In Jo's experience, the affective domain frequently matched the criteria of 'Not Achieving', 'Attention Needed', and 'Working Towards Outcomes' in her classes. To meet her goal of improving student relationships within her classes, Jo decided to use a variety of cooperative learning structures. She did this in the belief that learning in all domains would be enhanced as a result of a focus on the affective domain.

A rationale for using action research methodology

It would be easy (and yet disingenuous) to suggest, given Ash's knowledge of both cooperative learning and action research, that a combined approach to this study seemed the obvious fit. The truth is, the plan to explore teaching in the affective domain superseded Jo's interest in action research. That said, when Jo mentioned her wish to action some ideas around affective learning and explore it through a practitioner research project, Ash was happy to help and suggested action research. We met digitally (via applications such as Skype, Google Hangout and Voxer) and talked about the merits of different forms of practitioner research, but Ash's conclusion (see Casey, 2013) that steps and not just journeys are important in reporting on pedagogical change swayed our final methodological decision.

The research process using action research methodology

Participants and settings

Jo's research took place in a high school in Wisconsin, USA. The school has approximately 1400 students in grades 10–12 (years 11–13 in the UK) and Jo's research was focused on students who were in a physical education class called 'Fitness for Life'. The course was a core requirement for all students and comprised grade 10 students, with a handful of grade 11s in each class. Class sizes ranged from 21 to 29 for each of the four sections of the class. The Fitness for Life course presented Jo with an opportunity to see how successful different cooperative learning structures could be in promoting affective learning: both from one class to another and collectively.

Ethics

Due to the nature of our collaboration and Ash's distance from the school, it was decided to only gather data from Jo (either through her personal reflections or her reflections on conversations and interactions with others) and therefore no data were gathered directly from students, colleagues or the school. Formal ethical approval for the project was gained from Loughborough University.

Data gathering tools

Jo used post-teaching reflective analysis (PTRA) (Dyson, 1994) on a daily basis to reflect on and evaluate each lesson and determine how to move forward. Jo and Ash communicated via email, Skype, Google Hangout, Google Docs and Voxer. This allowed them to connect and discuss the process in real time despite being in different time zones. These meetings occurred regularly throughout the project with resources and ideas exchanged though the different online platforms. Ash's position as an external observer was helpful to Jo as he could draw on his experience to suggest different strategies in response to the various issues that arose during the research. Jo was also fortunate to have her colleague, Allisha, act in the role of critical friend. Jo also used student group rating scores, formative assessments, and both verbal and written student feedback to inform her personal reflections.

The action research cycle

The idea

The action research project occurred in two different classes engaged in the Fitness for Life course. Jo felt that these were classrooms in which the dynamics hindered the progress of many students:

> I had pockets of students in both classes, often different individuals from day to day, who were in one way, shape or form, adversely affecting the progress of all students. Problems ranged from contributing nothing to a group to putting other group members down or excluding them, intentionally or otherwise. Positive leadership was limited and there were a number of students who were more than content to be competent bystanders. In attempting to develop my students' problem solving and critical thinking skills, I didn't want to be a 'sage on the stage' teacher and therefore felt that creating an

environment where the students would need to positively depend on one another would help move the class forward.

(PTRA)

At the start Jo laid some groundwork by presenting her students with multiple opportunities to work cooperatively in a range of contexts and activities. For example, during a disc golf activity, students were asked to identify class norms they felt were required for the class as a whole, within smaller groups, and as individuals to be successful learners in physical education. Initially, each student identified positive and negative behaviours they had personally demonstrated in a physical education context and subsequently they created a personal improvement goal for working with others in the class.

Jo continued gathering data during a badminton unit. Along with skill development/refinement, tactics and strategic play, the unit targeted several grade level outcomes (SHAPE America, 2013) pertaining to the affective domain:

1   demonstrates positive interdependence when working as a team towards a common goal in badminton;
2   demonstrates problem solving skills and critical thinking skills, both as an individual and in groups;
3   exhibits proper etiquette, respect for others, and teamwork while engaged in physical activity; and
4   uses communication skills and strategies that promote team/group dynamics.

In what follows we have offered an insight into the action research process. These examples reflect the impact that different cycles of action research had on Jo over the course of the study. It is not definitive in any sense but is used to help the reader better understand how the cycle of think, plan, act, evaluate and reflect worked. It is important to note at this time that we haven't explicitly shown how Ash impacted Jo's thinking – there simply isn't room. We felt that this project was Jo's and that Ash served as an advisor and mentor but not as a researcher. We have done this to show how Jo, as a pedagogue, used action research to explore her own teaching.

Cycle 1

The timeline for each cycle varied and was determined by Jo's observations in class, her PTRA entries, and conversations with both Ash and Allisha. Cycle 1 took place over two 45-minute class periods.

Plan

With the thinking done (i.e. develop learning in the affective domain), my plan was to encourage my students to be comfortable with *not* knowing something and then seeking help from other students. Ultimately, I wanted them to use each other as a resource. I wanted to end 'competent bystanding' (Tousignant & Siedentop, 1983) and teach elements of the affective domain. In order to do this, I created hetero-geneous groups of 4–5 students. My goal was to have each group work together to complete their chosen warm-up tasks for the day and then make connections between those tasks and how they connected to skill-related and health-related fit-ness components. Additionally, I created 'Team Badminton Challenges' for each group to work through as a way to: (a) work cooperatively, and (b) think strategi-cally while (c) re-acquainting the students with how to play badminton.

Act

Independence and choice are two things I sought to embed in my instruction. I wanted students to arrive and immediately engage in warm-up activities that had purpose within the learning context. I developed a 'Badminton Bingo!' work-sheet where each square contained a warm-up activity specific to badminton that either focused on skill-related or health-related components of fitness. With previous classes I'd tasked my students with completing a set number of squares each day and, upon completion, to identify which skill- or health-related com-ponents each activity had addressed. While this approach worked for some stu-dents, those who weren't as self-directed or who struggled to make connections between the 'what' and the 'why' behind the activities didn't make the progress I'd anticipated.

The rationale behind placing students into warm-up/learning groups with parameters to follow (i.e. all activities must be completed as a group, each member of the group takes turns to choose the bingo activity square, the group discusses and makes a minimum of two connections between the activity and health-related and/or skill-related components of fitness) was to create a learning environment that positively impacted their affective learning. I felt this would build on work already done, particularly: being comfortable with not knowing something and using each other as a resource.

Evaluate

I reflected after each lesson and noted several positives early on:

> It was great to see discussion happening around which health-related compo-nent of fitness or skill-related component of fitness the students thought was being addressed. It was both a respectful and positive discussion. I'd empha-sised that more than one answer could be correct and the point of having these groups was to learn from different perspectives other than just our own as well as to draw on others' knowledge to strengthen the experience.
>
> (PTRA)

I created a worksheet for the team challenges so that each group could log their progress, reflect on how well they had done and when they had com-pleted a challenge. I noticed several verbal 'hurrahs' as teams completed a challenge – one student would be counting while another was making sure everyone knew who should be up next to take their turn.

(PTRA)

As a consequence of what I saw I decided to group four students in one class together. I reasoned that they would either sink or swim together:

> If they are in separate groups they disrupt others so I was hoping that if I put them together they would spend less time distracting others or looking to others for attention. Thankfully it worked. They still needed redirection but accepted it positively and worked together to complete the goal set. I think not having others to effectively bail them out helped.
>
> *(PTRA)*

Despite my best efforts to group my students to facilitate success, in each class there were one or two groups who failed to work cooperatively:

> I set up the groups again hoping to balance out students who are more easily distracted with those who I know are good at helping others stay on task. This is my smallest class and yet the hardest. One group was poles apart. The two girls were on task; the two boys wouldn't work or listen to the girls. I called them in and went over what they were aiming to accomplish and they reluctantly got back on task, after a couple of extra reminders.
>
> *(PTRA)*

Reflect

On observing the level of dysfunction that was occurring, I decided to make one immediate change. Group processing and reflection are both central steps in cooperative learning therefore I asked each student to rate their group's performance. My idea was that if each member rated the group's performance similarly, whether it was in need of improvement or not, it would mean they were at least on the same page. I had previously used Tuckman's (1965) stages of group formation (see Figure 6.1) to help the students recognise that it is normal for adversity to occur as a group progresses together.

Despite the use of Tuckman's model, it wasn't a case of trying something and seeing immediate results:

> Unsurprisingly the group who were not working together had scores all over the board. Groups who had worked well seemed to agree much more and more accurately on their performance as a group. I am planning to do this with every group/class now and track to see if the average score and spread changes as we move forward. I might also ask students to identify one thing they could do next time as an individual to improve the overall group performance.
>
> *(PTRA)*

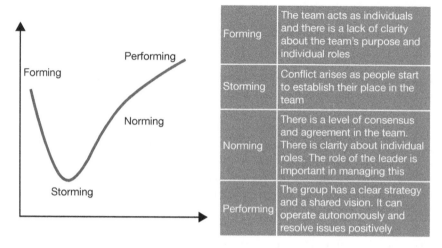

FIGURE 6.1 Tuckman's (1965) stages of group formation.

I also noted:

> I am torn between wanting to wait and see how it works and whether or not I should consider regrouping them now. At present, I'm erring on the side of leaving the groups be so I can see if they make progress or not. I also think if I disband dysfunctional groups now I'm sending the message that if something doesn't work we should make immediate changes rather than weather the storm.
>
> *(PTRA)*

Cycle 2

This second cycle of action research also occurred over two 45-minute class periods.

Plan

To facilitate greater positive interdependence and increase individual accountability I decided to create specific roles for each group member to fulfil: organiser, announcer, team motivator, quality controller and equipment manager. I gave each group a sheet detailing each role and asked them to record who was responsible for what. I felt it would also make it easier for me to keep a closer eye on what was/wasn't going well and diagnose the problem.

I also felt it would be beneficial to expand the group score tracking (posted on the wall for the students to refer to as they completed their group score for the lesson) to all groups/classes, both from a data perspective for me and as a reflection tool for the students.

Act

The roles helped significantly. I took time to explain each role, and how this system should help everybody, and provided guidance as to who in each group would be best suited to a particular role. I had a description of each role written on my whiteboard to add a visual as I talked to them.

The second part of the class centred on peer assessment which tasked the students with observing a member of their group to see: (a) if they were serving and scoring correctly or (b) if they were hitting to open space in the court. The primary function of this assessment was to get the students thinking more strategically about their movement and shot placement on court. However, by using peer assessment as a tool, I also felt I was creating a situation where affective learning would be important.

Evaluate

I reflected:

> Warm up participation and on task work was vastly improved in most of the classes – the roles given the previous lesson (organiser, equipment manager, quality controller, etc.) helped keep the group on task. I need to go over the worksheets to see how they are doing on making connections – I think many are only using 1–2 options (muscular endurance and cardio) rather than fully thinking them through.
>
> *(PTRA)*

In one class, peer assessment and communication were vastly improved. I had several conversations with different groups and many students said that by watching their peers, they understood better what they had to do within the game. In the smaller class we did not have the same success:

> I again had a small core of students who were disrupting their groups by not being on task. The rest of their group now seems resigned to ignoring them and staying on task themselves. I need to revisit this with these groups.
>
> *(PTRA)*

I did note, though, that the group scores for some groups were more in line with each other (i.e. all members of the group rated their work similarly). The group scores (how well the group worked together on a scale of 1–5, 1 being 'awful' and 5 representing 'really well') increased for some groups and as a collective the groups felt they were working better together.

Reflect

In one of our conversations I explained to Ash how differently the classes were responding to the structures I was using. He prompted me to consider the experiences the students were bringing with them to class, including the time of day of the class and who was in it. He asked me to consider how I might adapt to the school environment (i.e. our timetable means my more challenging class occurs over one of three lunch periods). This means some students have had lunch, while others haven't. I expressed my frustrations to Allisha and she suggested checking in at the beginning of the class with specific groups to reinforce the group's focus for the day with regards to working together, targeting one or two areas to really hone in on. We discussed targeting individuals within the groups and giving them a specific task to work towards for the betterment of the group (e.g. listening, being ready, or giving positive feedback).

I was pleased with the improvement in the court movement as a result of using peer assessment (i.e. by actively and purposefully watching their peers, and by giving feedback after each round). While the majority of the class were conscientiously trying to hit the shuttlecock into a space, even if it was not always successful, I did feel that each group would benefit from seeing themselves in action to further their development.

Cycle 3

Cycle 3 encompassed three 45-minute class periods.

Plan

Based on my conversations with Ash and Allisha, I decided to get the students playing badminton with whomever they wanted as soon as they were ready instead of getting immediately into their groups. My hope was that it would:

(a) give me an opportunity to check in with students in general and see how their day was going while giving them the opportunity burn off a bit of energy or discard any baggage from their previous classes;

(b) allow for other distractions to be taken care of (i.e. overlapping lunch periods); and

(c) allow me to speak to specific students or groups before they began their group work.

I wanted to use student roles more actively so that everyone would get more of a feel for how each person's role is integral to the group's success. To do this I set up an app called BaM video delay so that each group could see their court movement in action and reflect on it.

Act

I allowed 4–5 minutes of free hitting before getting the students into their groups to complete some more of their *Badminton Bingo* tasks. I asked each group's announcer to come and see me for directions for their group rather than talk to the whole class together. I did this specifically to challenge each group to think more broadly and use different health- or skill-related components to those they had already connected to activities.

I focused my iPad on one court, with the replay from the BaM video delay app displayed on a portable TV. I planned to move it from court to court as the students played and then have them go and review their play. I explained that we were aiming to build on the serving, scoring and court movement we'd tracked in the previous lesson by having each student see themselves playing and how well they were utilising the space on the court.

Evaluate

The free hit time was time well spent. I checked in with most of the students, especially those who had either been less engaged or who had been identified by both myself and by their peers as not contributing positively to the group. Having the announcers check in with me and then relay directions to their groups also worked out really well. I observed each group listening to their announcer and asking questions to clarify what was expected of them.

The video delay did not work out as I had planned:

> It was a distraction for some students initially who really just wanted to see themselves on camera. I did change its placement and had students view it when they rotated off the court. They did get to see some good placement but overall it didn't meet its intended means.
>
> *(PTRA)*

More positively, and for the first time, the group scores in a couple of the groups suggested they were working more affectively. The group who had been completely split on day one were now much more aligned in their group rating self-assessment. Each person in the group now assessed the group's performance as 'OK – we did work together but there is room for improvement' or higher. On chatting with the group, they all agreed that they had noticed an improvement but they were also honest in identifying something else they could individually do to bump up the group rating in the next class.

Reflect

Perhaps my biggest takeaway was how beneficial both structured and unstructured time can be. I am so conscious of maximising class time and ensuring students are on task that, at times, *I* probably contribute to them being off-task because I haven't provided time for my students to decompress and get mentally ready to learn in PE. I made a note to myself to take the temperature of each class as they arrive and adjust plans accordingly.

I did a much better job of utilising the roles in each group and I really enjoyed seeing students flourish as leaders within their specific roles. Moving forward, I think planning lessons with each role in mind will confirm every student's individual responsibility and help create more buy-in. I do think new ideas can bring value but I need to ensure they're not a distraction.

I am pleased with the group rating self-assessments and I've been tracking the average group score and the spread from day to day so I can see how this is changing. I need to make time for specific student reflections though and build in time for each group to make and record a goal for the next lesson.

A brief summary of the insights gained from using action research methodology

I entered into this research project with the intention of improving student learning in the affective domain. While I feel that I started to achieve this, I also felt it was an education into the messy process and continuous feedback loop that is action research. Seeing some groups move out of Tuckman's storming stage into the norming stage was hugely affirming for me. However, I now see Tuckman's model as more of a cyclical process where any group within a class may revisit stages within the model as the demands of an activity or type of activity change. The evaluation and reflection pieces within each cycle constantly challenged me to try new things because what worked in one situation didn't work in another. Despite Ash and I discussing this on numerous occasions, it still took a few cycles to really make sure that I kept messiness at the forefront of my mind when planning. There is no end to this process and there are really never any yes or no answers. Each day and each lesson provides information to use in planning for the next lesson. From a personal perspective, I know that I must build in more time and use more explicit instruction with regards to student reflection. It needs to be taught, modelled and reinforced if it is to serve its purpose, and my purpose, as a tool to develop the affective domain.

Moving forwards, I have realised that I am not the only one who benefits from an action research-style approach. My students also benefit greatly from the same process, with the result in this case being a more cohesive learning environment. I frequently observe my students focusing on 'what's next?' without using what they have experienced, learned and subsequently reflected on to determine their future steps. Therefore, I plan to extend the use of action research to include a student version, where the process will guide their learning pathway in each domain in PE.

References

Bailey, R., Armour, K., Kirk, K., Jess, M., Pickup, I., Sandford, R., & BERA Physical Education and Sport Pedagogy Special Interest Group. (2009). The educational benefits claimed for physical education and school sport: An academic review. *Research Papers in Education*, 24(1), 1–27.

Bloom, B.S. (1956). Taxonomy of educational objectives: The classification of educational goals. In M.D. Engelhart, E.J. Furst, W.H. Hill, & D.R. Krathwohl (eds), *Handbook 1: Cognitive domain*. New York: David McKay.

Casey, A. (In press). Cooperative learning and the affective domain. *JOPERD*.

Casey, A. (2013). 'Seeing the trees not just the wood': Steps and not just journeys in teacher action research. *Educational Action Research*, 21(2), 147–163.

Casey, A., & Goodyear, V.A. (2015). Can cooperative learning achieve the four learning outcomes of physical education? A review of literature. *Quest*, *67*(1), 56–72.

Dudley, D., Goodyear, V., & Baxter, D. (2016). Quality and health-optimizing physical education: Using assessment at the health and education nexus. *Journal of Teaching in Physical Education*, *35*(4), 324–336.

Dyson, B., & Casey, A. (2016). *Cooperative learning in physical education and physical activity: A practical introduction*. Abingdon, UK: Routledge.

Fernandez-Rio, J., Sanz, N., Cando, J.F., & Santos, L. (2017). Impact of a sustained cooperative learning intervention on student motivation. *Physical Education and Sport Pedagogy*, *22*(1), 89–105.

Hellison, D. (1987). The affective domain in physical education. *Journal of Physical Education, Recreation & Dance*, *58*(6), 41–43.

SHAPE America. (2013). *Grade-level outcomes for K-12 physical education*. Reston, VA: SHAPE America.

Tousignant, M., & Siedentop, D. (1983). A qualitative analysis of task structures in required secondary physical education classes. *Journal of Teaching in Physical Education*, *3*(1): 47–57.

Tuckman, B. (1965). Developmental sequence in small groups. *Psychological Bulletin*, *63*(6): 384–399.

Witt, P.L. (2015). Pursuing and measuring affective learning objectives. *Communication Education*, *64*(4), 505–507.

7

USING NARRATIVE INQUIRY IN PHYSICAL EDUCATION AND YOUTH SPORT

Reflecting on process

Brian Lewis and Lee Schaefer

With Sean Lessard[1]

Introduction

In this chapter we inquire into the process of a narrative inquiry research project. The project, which was titled 'A Narrative Inquiry into the Experiences of Urban Indigenous Youth in a Wellness Based After-school Program', took place over a three-year span and was a part of Brian's doctoral dissertation. At the beginning of the study Brian worked for a local school board as a physical education consultant and was also beginning his PhD course work. As a project team we were interested in what we might learn from providing holistic movement opportunities to urban Indigenous youth in a community setting. Given the ontological commitments of narrative inquiry (as described in Chapter 3), prior to framing this particular study it was important to engage in conversations with the community to ethically negotiate a research space that attended to the experiences of both the youth and the community. Brian was involved in this process of negotiation as well as in developing the research puzzle, study design, field text collection, conversations with youth mentors, the analysis of the field texts, the writing of the narrative accounts and the creation of a final research text. Through this chapter we hope to not only show the organic, and at times uncertain nature of this process, but also what Brian learned from engaging in the process of undertaking a narrative inquiry.

Situating the researcher within the research: Brian's autobiographical process

> This is my reflection time, pushing the dry mop up and down the gym floor before the programme begins. My time to think about today's plan, to wonder about the

---

1 Sean Lessard is one of the founders of the GYM project and provided valuable feedback on early drafts of this chapter. The authors would like to thank him for his contributions.

stories the kids will share in our circle, to consider how the programme has evolved in two short years. I take a moment to listen to the humming of the lights before the bell rings to end the school day which signals the beginning of our time together.

(Field text, 3 December 2014)

It may seem odd to start with a narrative fragment that is based on the autobiography of the researcher; however, a narrative inquirer's commitment to experience includes an attentiveness to how the researcher is situated within the research. Dewey's (1938) notion that experience is continuous and interactive means that for narrative inquirers, past experiences are continuously interacting with the research process; this includes the researcher's past experiences as well as those the researcher is conducting the narrative inquiry with. Therefore, it is imperative that narrative inquirers engage in extensive autobiographical work prior to beginning a narrative inquiry to better understand how they are situated within the research.

Brian notes: I begin with the field text in this section to symbolise that I always enter in the midst of experience (Clandinin & Connelly, 2000). My personal experience of sweeping a gymnasium floor is less about the actual act of pushing the broom and more about what I remember each time I clean the floors. Dewey's notions of continuity and interaction lead me to consider my past experiences as a teacher and curriculum consultant, experiences I had prior to beginning the inquiry. Clandinin (2013) reminds me that our lives as narrative inquirers – who we are and who we are becoming – are also under study. Thus, as I considered memories of pushing the broom as a teacher and as a member of an after-school programme I was able to travel temporally back and forth to understand experiences I have been part of that continue to shape my identity. The physical structure of a gymnasium has not changed in my last 19 years of teaching, but how it looks, feels and sounds certainly has.

Reflecting now on the research study I was part of, I see how crucial it was to inquire autobiographically. This self-facing, if you will, allowed me to begin to answer the proverbial questions around the significance of research – 'so what?' and 'who cares?' As Clandinin (2013) stated, 'without being clear about our responses to these questions of purpose and justification, we, as narrative inquirers, set ourselves up for that kind of simplistic reading of the research' (ibid., p. 35). It was through my autobiographical work that I began to justify the inquiry in three important ways: (1) personally, (2) practically, and (3) socially (ibid.). Furthermore, as well as attending to these justifications, I was able to make purposeful decisions around research puzzles, appropriate methods and field text collection, analysis and the conclusions of the research. In the section that follows I briefly illustrate how I conceptualised these justifications.

Darcy – personal justification

As we sat in my dimly lit basement classroom the feeling of unease encompassed me as I coveted to hear more about our new student Darcy other than his prognoses or downfalls. I was told little about Darcy other than he likely would not last a week. How do I prepare for this? It was suggested that I spend time reading through Darcy's cumulative file. Eventually I did, but it was not something I felt compelled to do from the onset. The meeting seemed to be a snap shot of that file, filled with scores, terminology, and shortfalls. I wanted to get to know Darcy for myself. I didn't want to welcome him into class with a perceived idea of what he was before I even met him.

(Field text, October 2013)

Shifting back temporally to the tension I felt many years ago listening to who Darcy was based on a cumulative file helps me to recognise how my thinking narratively came long before beginning doctoral studies. This starting point of beginning with definitions and prognoses, placed over the individual's experiences, was something I came to see as commonplace in other methodologies. Narrative inquiry as a methodology resonated on a personal level, allowing me to begin with the individuals I would be working alongside rather than the ideologies and frameworks prevalent in what would be considered dominant research paradigms.

Kelly – practical justification

Sitting at a local coffee shop, Sean, Lee, and I were putting the finishing touches on some planning for the programme. On this day, Barb, whom I had known for a number of years, stood in line for a coffee striking up conversation with our group. Barb was a counsellor at the neighbouring high school, the same school that Kelly was now attending as a grade nine student. I mentioned to Barb that Kelly was one of the employees of the programme and a tremendous asset. Her look of astonishment was telling. She questioned if we were talking about the same Kelly? She was in disbelief.

(Field text, January 2014)

As I considered the success Kelly experienced as a mentor in the programme and his struggles within school, I dwelled on the structure of high school, all the while reflecting on the graduation rates of Indigenous youth as compared to those of non-Indigenous youth within Saskatchewan. While Indigenous peoples comprise 15 per cent of the total provincial population, merely 25 to 30 per cent of Indigenous students complete high school within the typical three years it takes to advance from grade 10 through grade 12 (Saskatchewan Ministry of Education, 2009).

Joseph – theoretical/social justifications

I can't imagine how I survived the residential school[1] experience without some form of physical movement and education. I attribute the movement aspect ultimately to my survival and ability to go through the extreme traumatic events that occurred before and after the residential school experience.

(Field text, January 2017)[2]

Joseph is a humble, soft-spoken man who has taught me the need to slow down, to listen, and to come alongside the youth. Joseph continues to remind me of the importance of creating a connecting place for youth and reinforces my beliefs around building an inclusive community. Our time spent moving together in a gymnasium alongside the youth was a reminder for Joseph of early times playing outdoors with his peers. Joseph has helped me to see through his experiences; creating a sense of belonging is essential to establishing a mutual and respectful relationship alongside Indigenous youth. Through this inquiry alongside Indigenous youth, an opportunity arises for Indigenous and non-Indigenous peoples to find ways to move forward together at a time deemed by the Truth and Reconciliation Commission of Canada (TRCC) as 'a rare second chance' for reconciliation (TRCC, 2015, p. 113).

Background of the research

At the same time I was considering the personal, practical, and social justifications of this inquiry, I was also engaged in an extensive literature review. I saw it as crucial to understand what was prevalent within the literature when it came to after-school programming for Indigenous youth. As I worked through the literature I began to recognise common threads surfacing. These threads emerged as I noticed tensions with how Indigenous youth were depicted within the literature. The themes I came to see revolved around a conceptualisation of research done *on* Indigenous youth; themes that were imbued with notions of how after-school programmes could 'fix' youth who were in deficit.

I now see that recognising these themes came from both my past experiences living alongside students and the narrative inquiry lens that I was reading the literature through. When you enter into a study or read research with an ontological commitment to experience, you distinctly notice when others enter with epistemological frames that devalue experience. This lens allowed me to see that the youth were silent in the literature and were not positioned as knowledge holders. The tension felt from this positioning of youth was something that I needed to explore further as I continued to consider my research puzzle.

Identifying a research puzzle

Starting from an ontological commitment to experience, each narrative inquiry is composed around a particular wonder rather than thinking about framing a research question with expectations of a particular answer. Narrative inquirers frame a research puzzle that carries with it 'a sense of a search, a "re-search," a searching again . . . a sense of continual reformulation' (Clandinin & Connelly, 2000, p. 124). My autobiographical inquiry brought me to personally justifying this inquiry. Considering these justifications while moving through the literature review in turn brought me to thinking about a research puzzle. By thinking around a puzzle rather than a specific question, I remained committed to the experiences of the youth I was working alongside and my study became about better understanding their[3] experiences in an after-school programme based around wellness.

Negotiation of research space

As we shift back to our early conceptualisations of the research space, our intent was not to simply create an after-school programme *for* youth. We were intentional as narrative inquirers to ethically enter into a community, and to come alongside youth and families, to co-create a narrative inquiry research space. As narrative inquirers beginning with an interest in experience (Clandinin & Connelly, 2000), our commitments to inquiring alongside those within the programme proceeded from an ontological position, a curiosity about how people are living and the constituents of their experience. Our conceptualisation of this research space, in which all brought knowledge imbued with experiences (Clandinin, 1985), reminded us to move slowly and to listen to the community. As noted in the background of the research section, the majority of after-school programmes were designed as interventions (Halpern, 2002; Kremer, Maynard, Polanin, Vaughn & Sarteschi, 2015), looking to provide a potential solution to a problem. As narrative inquirers interested in experience, we saw the after-school programme not as an intervention but rather as a vehicle to begin to build relationships within a community.

It was important for us to begin to build relationships with a community that we did not live in. Ethically we were not comfortable entering into a research study without having taken the time to connect with the youth and the community. We spent time meeting with school administrators as well as members of the Parent Association to share our intentions of initiating an after-school programme. We were fortunate to connect with a community guide, Grandma Jean. As a member of the School Community Council, Jean provided insight into the needs of the community as well as connecting me to high school youth that would become mentors. We had also connected with a First Nation elder within the city who provided guidance with respect to the community I was entering in to.

In those initial weeks of the after-school programme we spent time talking with the high school mentors as well as the youth of the programme to hear what it was they would want to see in a programme. As we look back, we now see how we did a great deal of listening to how programming had previously existed in the community. We took time to hear what members of the community believed would work and what would not. With our ontological commitments to experience, we did not enter with a model or a clear path of programming. Rather, my focus was to allow community members to begin to know who we were. Taking this time speaks to the work of narrative inquiry and we believe helped to build trust with that community. The community members were able to see that we were interested in research *with the community* as opposed to *on the community*.

The research process

While the research process is always somewhat messy when beginning with onto-logical obligations to experience as the starting point, Clandinin and Connelly (2000), and more recently Clandinin (2013), identify key aspects that narrative inquirers need to be attentive to as they move through the research process. Given that there are entire books that attend to this process, in this chapter we specifically illustrate how Brian as both practitioner and researcher attended to the research processes that the aforementioned authors recommend.

Three-dimensional narrative inquiry space

Stories are just that until we spend time inquiring into them. As narrative inquirers, we need to remain awake to the three dimensions of place, temporality, and sociality. With each research participant, I was sure to continually inquire three-dimensionally into his or her experiences. Providing a brief example from one participant, Colin, I animate this process.

Inquiring into experiences Colin shared and narrative accounts he and I co-composed, I attended to the three commonplaces. Temporally speaking, Colin took me to experiences shared at home with his grandmother, to childhood memories of foster care prior to living with grandma, and to moments as a teenager in high school. These temporal moments shared shaped Colin's experience in the after-school pro-gramme as well as imagined future stories. In regard to place, I thought about how the gymnasium space, given Colin's athletic talents, has been a safe place, a place that has brought stories of success. These stories of safety and success were different from stories shared within Colin's larger community outside the after-school programme. These places helped me to think about the third commonplace of sociality. I thought about how Colin felt in these places, how larger social structures positioned him outside of the programme as an Indigenous youth thought to be in deficit.

As I moved through this inquiry, the three-dimensional space (place, temporality and sociality) constantly remained at the forefront. By inquiring into the stories shared, I was able to see the interconnectedness of the three-dimensional space.

Being in the field: practitioner, researcher or both?

From the inception of the study I was alongside youth and community in the field. All of my observations happened in the field during the programme and other programme time spent together. Sometimes these observations happened in the gymnasium setting, sometimes on a bus, and sometimes in another setting like the university; the line between practitioner and researcher becomes very blurry. In fact, like the other methodologies mentioned in this book, perhaps separating the two creates the notion that they cannot be done together, or that they are indeed separate entities. In this inquiry, like many narrative inquiries that take place in the field, the researcher was the practitioner and the practitioner was the researcher.

Ethical considerations

To engage deeply with experience is a relational commitment (Caine, Estefan & Clandinin, 2013) where ethical matters need to be considered over the duration of the inquiry. It is imperative to continually remain awake to the relational ethics. 'For those of us wanting to learn to engage in narrative inquiry, we need to imagine ethics as being about negotiation, respect, mutuality and openness to multiple voices' (Clandinin, 2006, p. 52). Our ethical commitments do not end with Research Ethics Board approval; quite the opposite, in fact. Throughout the narrative inquiry, we as researchers co-compose alongside participants moving from field texts to final research texts, always considering the lives we enter in the midst and eventually at some point exit.

Field to field texts

Clandinin and Connelly (2000) began using the term field texts as opposed to data, acknowledging how the work in the field is a co-composition that is reflective and experiential. These field texts are essentially records of this co-composition and may include field notes, transcripts of conversations, artefacts such as photographs or drawings, as well as writings (from both participant and researcher). How this looks is certainly contextual to the circumstances of the research space and participants. Clandinin (2013) points out that these field texts are diverse and it is important as researchers to stay awake to the multiple ways to tell and live experiences while continuing to keep the three-dimensional space in mind.

Specific to my inquiry, numerous field texts were developed and collected. At the conclusion of each week's programme, I entered a written reflection around my observations and experience in my journal (as shown in the opening vignettes) or reflected through a recorded dictation, which was then transcribed. These reflections varied, at times being centred on a short conversation with youth or from observations I made that seemed to resonate with me and the phenomenon under study. I also collected annals (intricate timelines) created by the participants and myself as we considered experiences within the programme. At times I would ask the youth to represent in a drawing or through text what the after-school programme meant to them. For example, how might they explain the programme to others? I also spent time with the youth mentors, talking about the experiences that have brought them and me to this programme and impacted our conceptualisation of topics such as wellness, school, community, and leadership, to name a few.

It was at this stage that I began to see the co-composition process within narrative inquiry taking shape. Field texts were not simply collected and created by me, the researcher, as would be the case using many other research paradigms. As the researcher, I saw the collection of field texts as something I did in conjunction with participants of the after-school programme. It is important to note, the vast collection of field texts developed over the first year of the inquiry was connected to many participants within the after-school programme prior to any decisions being made with respect to who in fact would be research participants.

After I completed my course work, and after about two years of being engaged in the programme, it became clear that I wanted to focus on the experiences of our three Indigenous high school mentors in the programme; Candace, Clary and Colin. I continued to compile field texts within the programme on a weekly basis, but began more in-depth research conversations with each of the three mentors. From April to June 2016, I engaged in five 90-minute conversations with each participant. While considering what I had come to know from the literature review, as well as my personal experiences within the programme, I sought to begin each research conversation by posing some of my own wonders connected to my initial research puzzles. The first research conversation centred on how the youth experienced school and how they saw our programme. In research conversation two, I was interested in hearing about the participants' experiences working with the youth within the programme. In the third conversation, I was interested in hearing what the participants thought about working with Indigenous youth from their community? Conversation four focused on the notion of knowledge. What knowledge did the participants bring to the programme that perhaps was not counted in other places? The final research conversation revolved around the notion of play and purposeful movement. Were the movement experiences within the programme similar or different from what the participants had experienced in other settings? All research conversations were recorded and transcribed verbatim.

Field texts to interim research texts

After the research conversations, I had to step away to consider the vast array of field texts collected while living alongside the participants. Detailed field texts support the transition to research texts, filling in the richness, nuances, and intricacies of the lived stories as well as the landscape (Clandinin & Connelly, 2000). Within many forms of research, this would be a time to analyse the data. From a narrative inquiry perspective, this is an opportunity to continue the co-composition process. 'Interim research texts are often partial texts that are open to allow participants and researchers opportunities to further co-compose storied interpretations and to negotiate the multiplicity of possible meanings' (Clandinin, 2013, p. 47). This was an opportunity for me to begin the process of writing 'narrative accounts' based upon the lived experiences in part with the participants as it related to the initial research puzzle(s).

> The term narrative account, or perhaps narrative accounting, allows us to give an account, an accounting, a representation of the unfolding of lives of both participants and researchers, at least as they became visible in those times and places where our stories intersected and were shared.
>
> *(Clandinin, 2013, p. 132)*

Co-composing the accounts involved time spent moving through initial drafts together. Through the negotiation we were able to co-create a representation of the 'unfolding of lives' (ibid.) that occurred over time spent together in and out of the after-school programme. As I thought across the three narrative accounts, and paid attention to 'resonances or echoes that reverberated across the accounts (ibid.), I simultaneously considered the three-dimensional narrative inquiry space. Threads identified included conceptualisations of play, school and education, community, as well as cultural narratives.

Interim research texts to final research texts

As narrative accounts were revisited through this three-dimensional lens, I could see more clearly the multiple meanings of experience. With the conclusion of the co-composition, final narrative accounts for each of the three participants were created by focusing on the aforementioned threads. This process was organic in nature, filled with a number of twists and turns along the way. There was not a linear approach to composing final research texts, as there was not one research question I was trying to answer. Clandinin (2013, p. 51) reminded me 'final research texts do not have final answers, because narrative inquirers do not come with questions'. The intent of these texts is to 'engage audiences to rethink and reimagine the ways in which they practice and the ways in which they relate to others' (ibid.). With the abundance of field texts collected over the years while coming alongside each participant, it was never my intent to try and compile all these experiences into a finding or an answer to a question. My intent was to try to represent the complexity of Candice's, Clary's and Colin's lives and experiences.

Considering the research puzzle, the justifications, as well as the literature I came to know through my review, I again looked across the narrative accounts for *resonances or echoes that reverberated*. I identified two resonant threads, common plotlines that appeared and reappeared over time and place in all three narrative accounts: (a) (re)conceptualisation of play and (b) (re)conceptualisation of community. These were two prevalent threads that I continued to inquire three-dimensionally while developing final research texts. As mentioned, only some of the field texts were shared in these final research texts. I selected field texts that supported these two resonating threads, texts that were part of the co-composition of narrative accounts. These chosen field texts helped to animate the tension between participants' lives and the dominant cultural and institutional narratives I had come to know, tensions that I shared in subsequent chapters of my dissertation.

What I learned about the process

By always returning to a commitment to experience as conceptualised by John Dewey (1938), I continue to see the uniqueness of this research methodology, gaining further understanding over time. This uniqueness brings with it a level of uncertainty that I became more comfortable with each day. I continue to be reminded of Clandinin's (2013) reference to Bateson who states, 'the knowledge developed from narrative inquiries is textured by particularity and incompleteness – knowledge that leads less to generalisations and certainties (Clandinin & Murphy, 2007) and more toward wondering about and imagining alternative possibilities' (Bateson, 2000, p. 52).

I learned that the two words *narrative* and *inquiry* come with a number of interpretations within the social sciences. How I came to understand narrative inquiry as conceptualised by Connelly and Clandinin (1990) was vastly different from other forms of narrative research. It was not as simple as hearing stories from research participants and then analysing to come to an answer of a predetermined research question. This inquiry was messy; it was filled with uncertainties and left me at times wondering if I was indeed on the correct path, or if there was a correct path. I learned that the messiness and uncertainty were necessary if I truly was interested in understanding youth's experiences.

I have come to understand just how we understand the word *research* and what that means to each of us. The dominant discourse within research revolves around words such as *validity* and *rigor*. Depending on phrases such as verisimilitude or trustworthiness, as I did, requires a much more detailed account of how the study took place, as well as how decisions were made. I learned that this process is easier said than done and that when others ask how decisions around analysis are made, it takes a great deal more attentiveness and time to describe.

That being said, I learned too that the ambiguity that stems from a commitment to experience brought with it a narrative understanding of experience. This inquiry was much more than the sharing of stories. From my experiences in doctoral studies, I was often challenged by others' perceptions around narrative inquiry as being nothing more than story telling. From my experiences moving through this inquiry, I see just how rigorous this methodology is. The process is time consuming: i.e. taking the time to build relationships, taking the time to ethically co-construct narrative accounts and final research texts that represent experiences shared. This taking time and moving slow bumped with the dominant narrative in research (Schaefer, Lessard & Lewis, 2017). I could have easily gone into an after-school programme, measured something and left. I would have found data to answer a question posed, leaving me to summarise the findings. This I know now would have left me feeling that I was a 'researcher of' as opposed to a 'researcher with'. This captures a significant difference in approaching research when it comes to thinking about building relationships with Indigenous youth, families, and community. I learned that for me narrative inquiry was a methodology that was integral in coming to know others and building relationships.

Notes

1 Residential schools were government sponsored religiously based schools that were designed to assimilate Indigenous individuals into Western society. The TRCC was created as a way to provide actionable items to work towards reconciliation between Indigenous and non-Indigenous individuals. The intergenerational trauma from residential school experiences continues to live on in many communities.

2 This text was part of a written story Joseph shared with me. As negotiated, Joseph gave me permission to use an excerpt of his story.
3 This inquiry looked at the experiences of three youth mentors within the programme: Candice, Clary, and Colin.

References

Bateson, M. C. (2000). Pragmatising the curriculum: Bringing knowledge back into the curriculum conversation, but via pragmatism. *The Curriculum Journal, 25*(1), 29–49.

Caine, V., Estefan, A., & Clandinin, D. J. (2013). A return to methodological commitment: Reflections on narrative inquiry. *Scandinavian Journal of Educational Research, 57*(6), 574–586.

Clandinin, D. J. (1985). Personal practical knowledge: A study of teachers' classroom images. *Curriculum Inquiry, 15*(4), 361–385.

Clandinin, D. J. (2006). Narrative inquiry: A methodology for studying lived experience. *Research Studies in Music Education, 27*(1), 44–54.

Clandinin, D. J. (2013). *Engaging in narrative inquiry.* Walnut Creek, CA: Left Coast Press.

Clandinin, D. J., & Connelly, F. M. (2000). *Narrative inquiry: Experience and story in qualitative research.* San Francisco, CA: Jossey-Bass.

Clandinin, D. J., & Murphy, S. (2007). Looking ahead: Conversations with Elliot Mishler, Don Polkinghorne, and Amia Lieblich. In D. J. Clandinin (ed.), *Handbook of narrative inquiry: Mapping a methodology* (pp. 632–650). Thousand Oaks, CA: Sage Publications.

Connelly, F. M., & Clandinin, D. J. (1990). Stories of experience and narrative inquiry. *Educational Researcher, 19*(5), 2–14.

Dewey, J. (1938). *Experience and education.* New York: Collier.

Halpern, R. (2002). A different kind of child development institution: The history of after-school programs for low-income children. *Teachers College Record, 104*(2), 178–211.

Kremer, K. P., Maynard, B. R., Polanin, J. R., Vaughn, M. G., & Sarteschi, C. M. (2015). Effects of after-school programs with at-risk youth on attendance and externalizing behaviors: A systematic review and meta-analysis. *Journal of Youth and Adolescence, 44*(3), 616–636.

Saskatchewan Ministry of Education. (2009). *Inspiring success: Building towards student achievement.* Regina: Saskatchewan Ministry of Education. Retrieved from http://publications.gov.sk.ca/documents/11/89498-Inspiring%20Success%20final.pdf

Schaefer, L., Lessard, S., & Lewis, B. (2017). Living tensions of co-creating a wellness program and narrative inquiry alongside urban aboriginal youth. *LEARNing Landscapes.*

TRCC. (2015). *Truth and reconciliation commission of Canada: Calls to action.* Winnipeg, Manitoba: Truth and Reconciliation Commission of Canada. Retrieved from www.trc.ca/websites/trcinstitution/File/2015/Findings/Calls_to_Action_English2.pdf

8

USING AUTOETHNOGRAPHY TO EXPLORE A CULTURE OF SCHOOL SPORT

Jodi Harding-Kuriger and Doug Gleddie

Introduction

This chapter explores the development of a collaborative autoethnographic research project. The work began as a final assignment for a graduate studies class entitled 'Reflective Practice in Education' at the University of Alberta. The course examined four methodologies and enabled students to explore the ways each methodology resonated with their own context and identity. In consultation with the instructor (Doug), the culminating project allowed the student (Jodi) to choose and explore a way to use one or more of the methodologies for reflective practice in their own context. Jodi's autoethnographic project became the foundation for our work here.

The purpose of this chapter is to demonstrate the process of a collaborative autoethnography (Chang, Wambura Ngunjirir, & Hernandez, 2013) from start to finish. Beginning with Jodi's initial idea and the decisions that went into it, we will move into the creation of a research/ reflective question(s), selection and refine-ment of artefacts, process of analysis and collaboration, expository of findings and, finally, the impact of this study on Jodi's ongoing role as a teacher–coach. As we take the reader along with us on this journey, we hope to provide an inside look at the 'why', 'what' and 'how' of autoethnography as a way to conduct reflective practice in coaching.

Introductions of the practitioner, the context and the researcher

My coaching identity has transformed incredibly over the past 16 years. I started by coaching U6 soccer with a friend of mine. We had no clue what we were doing: no philosophy, rare practice plans and no seasonal goals. Mostly, we did it just to volunteer (and to help our resumes!). Our sessions generally started out with running laps for a warm up (my heart breaks), drills and skills (my heart is seriously aching now), and then a big scrimmage involving the entire team or a game against another U6 team. The 'athletes' would be somewhat engaged. Some chased the ball, some picked flowers and some did gymnastics on the goal posts. Even back then I think I knew I was not a great coach. Therefore, although I played a lot of sports, I did not coach again until I started teaching.

Of course, I then jumped in with both feet! I coached anything and everything they told me to. Thankfully my first team was a junior high (grades 7–9) girls' soccer team. I co-coached with another new teacher. We had a blast! We were both soccer players, we loved to laugh and we loved the girls. Our practices consisted of running warm ups, drills, strategy games, and scrimmages. During games, it was not uncommon to see one of us running alongside the play with our girls, coaching them as they moved down the field. We were having fun, they were having fun, and we were winning. In fact, we won the City Championship our second year coaching that team.

As I changed schools I continued to coach. During job interviews I was asked very few questions about my physical education teaching philosophy or my commitment to physical literacy. The selling feature always seemed to come back to, 'How will you contribute to athletics and what will you coach?' These past fifteen years of my teacher–coach life I feel I have not been reflective enough. These years have been a whirlwind of teaching, coaching, parenting and learning (in that order). It was time to slow down, stop, and take a critical look back.

Statement of the research problem/ question/aim that is being explored

In Canada, physical education teachers, especially at high school, are often hired for their coaching ability rather than their teaching ability. In fact, the Health and Physical Education Council in Alberta has a position statement explicitly opposing that practice (HPEC, 2017). It seems like being a good physical educator is not enough. You also need to coach. That is the cultural expectation: 'Whether learners view physical education [and school sport] as inclusive and supportive of all participants or as predominantly technical and elitist depends greatly on the routine experiences they have of this subject' (Prain & Hickey, 1995, p. 88). The focus on coaching and sport minimises the role of physical education pedagogy. If young people see that their teachers (parents, principals) really only care about physical activity for 'elite' athletes – the chosen few – it sends the wrong message about physical education and those that teach it.

Aims of the research

As we discussed our common experiences as teachers and coaches, we sought a focus for Jodi's project. We decided that autoethnography as reflective practice would be an excellent method to focus on her relationship with the culture of school sport during the pivotal years when Jodi set up a school sport programme in a new school. As such, we can begin to see the pressures and expectations through Jodi's eyes as she negotiates the spaces of and between physical education teacher, coach, and athletic director. Jodi chose autoethnography not for its ability to produce objective findings but for its desire to 'challenge what counts as knowledge' (Morimoto, 2008, p. 31). Her autoethnographic account can serve as a way of better knowing the teacher–coach within the school sport culture (Hamdan, 2012). Our goal is to share Jodi's experience to see deeper into the culture of school sport and teacher–coaches. In this way, she is able to use her present understanding of physical education, coaching and school sport to analyse and assess her past decisions. Overall, we want to 'study culture's relational practices, common values and beliefs, and shared experiences for the purpose of helping insiders (cultural members) and outsiders (cultural strangers) better understand the culture' (Ellis, Adams, & Bochner, 2011, p. 275). Specifically, we want to dig deeply into:

- The decisions Jodi made in that year and the pressures and expectations surrounding school sport culture.
- Her learning from this approach to reflective practice and how it can impact her decisions today and in the future.
- How this journey can be impactful to both insiders (coaches, players, students) and outsiders (parents, principals, trustees) in the creation of effective school sport culture.

A rationale for using autoethnographic methodology

'Autoethnography is an approach to research and writing that seeks to describe and systematically analyze personal experience in order to understand cultural experience' (Ellis, Adams & Bochner, 2011, p. 273). This quote is at the heart of what we seek to do with this project. We are using Jodi's personal experiences to understand further the pressures, expectations and experiences of that particular culture. Our work also aligns with the foundational assumptions of autoethnography (Chang, 2008) examined in Chapter 4.

First, as we explore Jodi's artefacts and experiences, we are immediately connected to the others within her context. Colleagues, administrators, students and parents: all are part of the culture and connected to Jodi's story of self (and concept of culture). Chang (2008) also proposes a concept of culture, albeit a work in progress, that will be helpful to our understanding of the culture of school sport (Table 8.1).

Second, through Jodi's autoethnography we are able to develop an appreciation of her context and experiences. As well, her narrative of self connects us to the multiple others who share her culture and can lead to a deeper, more holistic understanding. Thirdly, it is not enough to simply tell stories or share artefacts. We need to analyse and interpret the culture of school sport through Jodi's

TABLE 8.1 Chang's (2008, pp. 21–23) concept of culture as applied to Jodi's context.

According to Chang	According to Jodi
Individuals are cultural agents, but culture is not all about individuality.	School sport culture certainly has individual diversity; however, Jodi and other individuals act as representatives of a collective culture.
Individuals are not prisoners of culture.	Despite being a representative, Jodi is able to interchange cultural traits as she interacts with others – within and without.
Despite inner-group diversity, a certain level of sharedness, common understanding, and/or repeated interactions is needed to bind people together as a group.	Common understandings such as a belief in 'elite athletics' and 'winning' can act to connect members of a culture through their repetition and perceived importance.
Individuals can become members of multiple social organisations concurrently.	Jodi is a female, a physical education teacher, a mother, a coach and a graduate student – all at the same time.
Each membership contributes to the cultural makeup of individuals with varying degrees of influence.	Depending on her context, Jodi's identity and affinity with her multiple social constructs can wax and wane accordingly.
Individuals can discard a membership of a cultural group with or without 'shedding' their cultural traits.	Jodi can become an athletic director, but her physical education teacher traits will remain a part of her identity.
Without securing official memberships in certain cultural groups, obvious traits of membership, or members' approvals, outsiders can acquire cultural traits and claim cultural affiliations with other cultural groups.	Although she may define herself first as a physical education teacher, Jodi can gain acceptance and affiliation with coaches through adopting some of their cultural traits.

experience in order to begin the journey of understanding. Finally, we seek to use this methodology for instruction and learning for practitioners (teacher–coaches, athletic directors) within the culture of school sport. The intent is for others involved in similar cultures to read and think about Jodi's story and analysis and begin to gain a deeper understanding of their own context and complex web of relationships.

The research process using autoethnographic methodology

Our work fits into the collaborative sphere of autoethnography for several reasons. As a two-person team, our research relationship is based on prior shared experiences and collaboration. Even though our most recent interactions have been as a student and a professor, in the past we have co-chaired a conference together and served on numerous committees in equal roles. These prior interactions have helped build a respectful relationship that allows us to go beyond the potential power dynamic of student–professor to genuinely collaborate on this project.

We also chose to go the route of full collaboration; however, methodologically we are blending aspects of conversation, collaboration and duoethnography. Although the artefacts and autobiographical sharing is Jodi's alone, Doug engaged in extensive conversations, research and analysis with Jodi based on his experiences as a teacher–coach and athletic director in similar cultural situations. Autoethnography, as discussed in Chapter 11, is a methodology in which ethical responsibilities can be satisfied informally, formally or sometimes in both ways. For this work, Jodi used an informal approach to ethics and took a number of steps to ensure consent (Jodi is the only participant), confidentiality (pseudonyms, detail changes, care for colleagues) and transparency (Jodi and I worked together openly – no deception occurred). In this way, although a formal application to an ethics review board was not required, Jodi is still engaged in ethical research.

Data

As in ethnography, there is value and strength in using a variety of data sources for autoethnography. The first step in the data gathering process was for Jodi to identify and refine a collection of self-narratives and artefacts to study. She began by reflecting back to key events from her teaching-coaching life when she truly questioned the rationale for the school sport culture. These 'critical incidents' were 'times of existential crises that forced [me] to attend to and analyze lived experience' (Ellis, Adams, & Bochner, 2011, p. 275). The narratives are based on actual events, and are taken from Jodi's personal diary; however, names and some identifying details have been changed in the interest of anonymity. Figure 8.1 is a timeline that provides temporal perspective for the data.

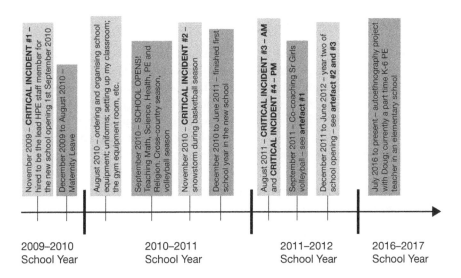

FIGURE 8.1 Timeline of Jodi's autoethnography.

Critical incident 1: November 2009

I got the job! I actually got the job! This is amazing that Penny and Bernadette chose me. I am going to be the Health and Physical Education (HPE) Lead teacher for the new school. What an incredible opportunity. They chose a single, pregnant woman with barely five years of teaching experience! I will be leading the staff in all things HPE, Athletics, Sport, and Intramurals. We are going to have a team in every single sport in our opening year! New fresh uniforms! Imagine if we won a City Championship in our inaugural year! Now THAT would show them! We will only have one gym for 812 students. So juniors will have to practice in the mornings, seniors after school. Intramurals for all grades at lunch. I'll have to create a big calendar schedule for everyone. THIS IS GOING TO BE AWESOME!

Critical incident 2: Late November 2010

What have I done?! This is insane. It is 8pm at night. There is a snowstorm blowing in. We are at least an hour from home. My 10-month-old, gym-rat son is starving, tired and cranky. And yet here we are, sitting on the cold floor of a darkened hallway, waiting. Waiting for one of my senior boys basketball players to be picked up from our away game, which ended more than 2 hours ago. We have tried and tried to reach Leonard's family, but no answer. He is sitting there looking so sorry and he is really trying to keep Aidan entertained by playing catch with him. I should have just driven him home. Screw the district policy. What other 'profession' does this much extra work and puts in this much extra time after work? What have I done?

Critical incident 3: Early morning – prior to THAT August staff meeting 2011

Another incredible opportunity! Assistant Principal (AP) in our school! Everything just keeps getting better and better for me. I am halfway done my Masters of Education (M.Ed) degree. This is going to be another great year. I'll be putting my M.Ed. theory into practice. I'll really get to be a leader and role model for my fellow staff. I'll get to teach Math and PE part time, and the rest of the time I'll be in the office. I may even get to coach a little less. That'll be great for Aidan and I.

Critical incident 4: Late afternoon – after THAT August staff meeting 2011

Up, down, up, down, up, and down. Those are my emotions all the time at work. Our poor junior high teachers did not seem as excited or pumped for the year as I had hoped. Between the six of us I thought we would have no problems dividing up the junior high athletics. Cross country, volleyball × 4 teams (junior & senior boys and girls), basketball × 4 teams, badminton, curling, Track & Field, and slow pitch. I offered to coach five out of thirteen of them. If everyone else coached or helped with 2, or if we got some elementary teacher help, then all the teams would be covered. No problem, right? Maybe we will have to drop some teams this year? Who designed a new school so small? We will make this work. This is a good administrative challenge for me. Right? Or did I get it all wrong. Last year Penny cautioned me against moving so quickly – slow down, let the teams and the school grow with time. I remember feeling frustrated with her. She had trusted me to lead the school but then it seemed she was trying to stop me. I was wrong. I had something to prove. I wanted our school to be out of the starting gates in the lead excelling in athletics excellence, students healthy and active after-school. Even though it has meant hauling Aidan into the gym almost every day after school. Even though it has meant exhausting our junior high staff. Even though it has mean depleting the 30 athletes that play everything. Even though it has meant exhausting myself. How much more time in the gym can my 18-month old baby and I endure? It is going to be a long year and it is only August. What have I done?

Of course, Jodi had a plethora of memories and incidents to choose from. We first discussed this time in her life and our research objectives. As we spoke, we began to narrow down these key moments based on the timelines we wished to explore and the passion/intensity of the events. Doug listened for those times when it seemed like Jodi was especially invested in the moment or had a strong emotional attachment. Over several conversations, we began to narrow down the 'critical incidents' and Jodi worked to write and flesh out her narratives including the four shared above.

In addition to these narratives, Jodi also dug through her files to find artefacts of the school sport culture she was a part of. Relevant artefacts could include lesson plans, student or parent letters, awards, pictures, etc. Again, we started with a larger list of items that we discussed and narrowed down to the ones that elicited the most investment and impact. Artefact 1 was a school-based 'form' that all athletes had to share with their parents, read and sign. We chose to use this artefact because it is indicative of the school sport culture that existed in Jodi's school. It provides clear evidence of the philosophies that Jodi, her team of coaches and the school bought into.

Artefact 1: excerpt from senior girls volleyball form

Team Goals

As a team we have set our goals as the following:

1   Season Goal: We would like to make it to the semi-finals.
2   Tournament Goals: We would like to compete in the finals in all our tournaments.

To achieve these goals we have established a team philosophy:

1   Season Philosophy: We will play with a starting 6 (plus libero) line up. We will only be making changes if there is injury or we have a significant lead in points or are up 2 sets to nothing.
2   Tournament Philosophy: Everyone will have equal playing time during tournaments.

Expectations

All student athletes are expected to:

- Demonstrate commitment to their responsibilities as a student first.
- Maintain or exceed the expectations of classroom teachers and coaches as reviewed throughout the year by the staff. (i.e., homework, punctuality, preparedness, consistent effort.)
- Be positive role models, promoting our 'core values' as ambassadors of the school both on and off site.

Artefacts 2 and 3 provide a counterpoint to the volleyball form. While engaged in her archaeological dig, Jodi unearthed two cards from her former students (Figures 8.2 and 8.3). We immediately agreed that these cards should be part of the

FIGURE 8.2 Artefact 2: card from a student.

FIGURE 8.3 Artefact 3: card from a student

study because of their counter-cultural nature. These were not cards from players or parents of players but, rather, from 'average' students in Jodi's PE classes. These artefacts reminded Jodi of the type of kids that get missed in the culture of elite school sport and how important they are to the fabric of the school. We included them to help us reflect on and seek to understand the complexity and diversity of a school's created culture of movement and physical activity.

Data analysis

After confirming and refining the data sources for this study, we engaged in a reflective and collaborative analysis of the data. As stated earlier, the context we are exploring is Jodi's. Given the nature of our collaboration the analysis shared below is presented from Jodi's perspective; however, Doug engaged with the data as well from his parallel experiences as a teacher–coach and athletic director. Together we engaged in a process of data analysis that involved reading, reflecting, discussing and revising.

Critical incidents 1 and 2

This was the very first time that I truly began to question the teacher–coach life-style. Up to this point I had always loved coaching and knew that the relationships

I built with my students through coaching were valuable. The extra time spent with those students really allowed us to get to know each other. These relationships were also invaluable in the classroom. My student–athletes were comfortable asking questions, leading group discussions, and demonstrating both success and failure during new activities. They were comfortable with me and trusted that I would teach them in a safe and caring way.

However, at what cost to my entire classroom? What about the other students? I did build rapport with them as well and they knew I cared about their learning. But we were not as close. We did not share as many jokes or smiles. Is this fair? The extra time coaching also meant that I had less time for planning and preparation. Could I have been a better teacher if I had spent fewer hours coaching and more time reflecting and planning? I truly believe I could have. This teacher–coach lifestyle also came with a cost to my family. My son was hauled around from practice to practice, game to game, tournament to tournament. He was only 10 months old, but I am sure that he could feel that I had put my student–athletes before him most weeknights and some weekends.

Artefact 1

As a coaching team, we *loved* those kids, we told them often, and we showed it to them. We earned our student–athletes' respect because our coaching 'strategies included the development of an expert persona', we were 'in control of events', we 'knew what [we] were doing, while also portraying an understanding, caring image of having the athletes' best interests at heart' (Purdy et al., 2008, p. 331). When I look back at this form for student–athletes there is some value in it, but there is also some danger. As a coach, I feel that the *team* needs to set goals and philosophies. It allows for clear expectations and procedures during the season. As a teacher, I think that students need to commit to their studies first and their sport second.

The danger lies in the premise that this was a competitive sport. It was *grade 7–9 volleyball*! According to the Canadian Sport for Life, Long Term Athlete Development model, these kids were in Stage 4: Train-to-Train:

> The Train-to-Train stage makes or breaks the athlete. Athletes may exhibit special talent, play to win, and do their best, but they still need to allocate more time to training skills and physical capacities than competing in formal settings. To maximise their long-term potential, winning should remain a secondary emphasis.
>
> (*Canadian Sport for Life, 2016, no page number*)

There it is, plain and simple. A recreational intramural programme would have suited them much better. We could have been following a Teaching Games for Understanding (TGfU) (Griffin & Butler, 2005) approach to net and wall games. Many more students would have been able to participate instead of just the 'starting 6 line-up'. It would have been much more beneficial for their overall health, well-being and physical literacy to have engaged all students in a more recreational and developmental version of school sport. There was little evidence to support the competitive athletic culture I created.

Artefacts 2 and 3

These cards both came from boys in my PE class that were not student–athletes. Each was from a different ethnic group, neither had the stereotypical 'athlete' body and one was diagnosed on the Autism spectrum. I am so glad that I was able to keep them healthy and make them feel awesome. To better serve students like these, and the rest of the eight hundred plus students of the school, I wish I had not pushed for competitive athletic teams to begin with. It would have been much better to begin with intramural programmes after school for all students – kindergarten through grade 9. This would have given me the time and space to increase the 'motivation, confidence, physical competence, knowledge and understanding' (Whitehead, 2010, p. 11) of *all* students. This is what quality physical educators should be doing. It should be the focus of our curricular programming and our extracurricular endeavours. In this I failed to take a risk and I fell back to what all junior high schools were *supposed* to do – compete in all the athletic seasons.

Critical incidents 3 and 4

Not only had my athletic fever infected my family, but also my friends and co-workers. This was unacceptable. I had been given the opportunity to really make a difference in the lives of students and staff and I had failed. Research shows that 'a growing number of experts in the field of PE have been arguing that physical education's resistance to change poses a serious problem' (Cameron, 2012, p. 4). I had become a part of that problem. I had perpetuated the teacher–coaching lifestyle, which is not always a healthy one.

These incidents also demonstrated how I had alienated the vast majority of the students from physical activity during the critical hours after school. According to the ParticipACTION Report Card on Physical Activity, 'However, as the guidelines change to 60 minutes of moderate- to vigorous-intensity physical activity per day for those aged 5 to 17, only 9% are meeting the guidelines' (ParticipACTION, 2016, p. 4). I was contributing to their inactivity by not being innovative and proactive. I was perpetuating a competitive sporting culture, not a healthy school community.

A brief summary of the insights gained from using autoethnography methodology

'As an ethnographer I should be trying to do something more than 'just tell a good story', to break readers' hearts, or to understand myself in deeper ways' (Ellis & Bochner, cited in Purdy et al., 2008, p. 323). Rather, I should also be trying to do something that is critical; something that tries to explain to myself and others 'the socially organised powers in which our lives are embedded and to which our activities contribute' (Smith, cited in Purdy et al., 2008, p. 323). Teachers' lives are embedded in their work. We invest ourselves fully in our classrooms, in our planning, in our delivery and in our relationships with our students. As a teacher–coach, we take this one step further. We give even more of our time and energy to our students before and after school. We feel obligated to coach teams so that kids can be active, generate school spirit and build camaraderie.

These are all good things. I love physical activity, I love to move, and play, and sweat. As a teacher–coach I did all of these things with my student–athletes but often at the expense of the other students. I wish I could do it all over again, only now I would not push for teams right away. My process would be much more organic and slow. I would focus on recreation and participation for all students in the school. Before and after school the gym would not be solely for teams. There would be balance.

Bailey et al. found the following:

> the importance of establishing secure movement foundations for participation and performance, together with the health imperative to engage young people in lifelong learning for lifelong engagement in physical activity, are resulting in gradual changes to PESS (Physical Education and School Sport) programs.
>
> *(Bailey et al., 2009, p. 9)*

More research is needed in the field of education around the teacher–coach culture and the perceived benefits of school sport. These moments of existential crises, of identity construction and reconstruction have been articulated through autoethnography. This critical reflection '[acknowledged] the inextricable link between the personal and cultural' (Wall, 2006, p. 2). There exists a cultural expectation that all PE teachers also coach. There is institutional support for the teacher–coach culture (Cameron, 2012), including incentives and 'perks' such as prep blocks and exemptions from staff meetings.

This predominant culture shaped my identity for many years. I was young, scared, and naive. I went along with the coaching crowd and did not question established expectations. Now as I learn more about physical literacy and long-term athlete development I really wonder if the competitive coaching culture should be so dominant. Philosophically, the teacher–coach lifestyle no longer aligns with my values and beliefs. I value time with my growing family. I value time to prepare and plan for my PE courses. I value physical activity for all. It is time to put my story and learning into action.

The academic review conducted by Bailey et al. truly resonated for me when they asked, 'for which educational benefits could – or should – physical education [and school sport] be held accountable?' (Bailey et al., 2009, p. 16). Their findings indicated that there is a need for more research and that the research should be influencing both our praxis and practice. As pedagogues, we need 'to have an impact on enhancing young people's physical activity levels in order to improve their health, then it could be argued that some current practices should be discontinued because they do not appear to 'work' for many young people' (ibid., p. 17). Comprehensive school and community health is where our experts in PE should be focusing their time. The teacher as coach expectation is not the answer. The entire school community needs to be involved to ensure *all* kids can be healthy and active.

Jodi's reflections on the research process

My autoethnography focused primarily on my personal experiences (*auto*) in an attempt to shed some light on the existing teacher–coach culture in schools (*ethno*) (Ellis, Adams, & Bochner, 2011). My teacher–coach identity was very much shaped by my mentor teacher–coaches in schools. Only as I pursued graduate studies and professional development opportunities did I begin to truly see what we were missing as educators. My stories and artefacts will hopefully provide interrogation and critique for all educators (Morimoto, 2008). Kirk challenges us:

> if quality physical education is our aim, then we must scrutinise what currently goes on in the name of physical education practices . . . We must then formulate and advocate vigorously for forms of physical education that are specific to human interests and needs of young people within specific, local contexts.
>
> *(Kirk, cited in Bailey et al., 2009, p. 18)*

Finally, this work is my cry for reform in the school sport culture, especially for pre-service teachers. Consider these teacher–coaching challenges and what they might mean for you. To my students and players, this is my thoughtful apology and a promise to be a better teacher–coach.

References

Bailey, R., Armour, K., Kirk, D., Jess, M., Pickup, I., Sandford, R., & BERA Physical Education and Sport Pedagogy Special Interest Group. (2009). The educational benefits claimed for physical education and school sport: An academic review. *Research Papers in Education*, 24(1), 1–27.

Cameron, E. (2012). DE/REconstructing my athlete–student–teacher self: A critical autoethnography of resistance in physical education teacher education (PETE). *PHEnex Journal*, 4(2), 1–9.

Canadian Sport for Life. (2016). Long term athlete development plan. Retrieved from: http://sportforlife.ca/train-to-train.

Chang, H. (2008). *Autoethnography as method*. Walnut Creek, CA: Left Coast.

Chang, H., Wambura Ngunjiri, F., & Hernandez, K. (2013) *Collaborative autoethnography*. Walnut Creek, CA: Left Coast.

Ellis, C., Adams, E., & Bochner, A. (2011). Autoethnography: An overview. *Historical Social Research*, *36*(4), 273–290.

Griffin, L., & Butler, J. (2005). *Teaching games for understanding: Theory, research, and practice*. Champaign, IL: Human Kinetics.

Hamdan, A. (2012). Autoethnography as a genre of qualitative research: A journey inside out. *International Journal of Qualitative Methods*, *11*(5), 585–606.

HPEC. (2016). *School athletics – John Semkuley*. Edmonton, Alberta: Health and Physical Education Council. Retrieved from www.hpec.ab.ca/position-papers.

Morimoto, L. (2008). Teaching as transgression: The autoethnography of a fat physical education instructor. *Proteus*, *25*(2), 29–36.

ParticipACTION. (2016) *Report card on physical activity for children and youth*. Toronto: ParticipACTION. Retrieved from www.participaction.com/sites/default/files/down loads/2016%20ParticipACTION%20Report%20Card%20-%20Highlight%20Report. pdf.

Prain, V., & Hickey, C. (1995). Using discourse analysis to change physical education. *National Association for Physical Education in Higher Education*, *47*, 76–90.

Purdy, L., Potrac, P., & Jones, R. (2008). Power, consent and resistance: An autoethnography of competitive rowing. *Sport, Education and Society*, *13*(3), 319–336.

Wall, S. (2006). An autoethnography on learning about autoethnography, *International Journal of Qualitative Methods*, *5*(2), 2–12.

Whitehead, M. (2010). *Physical literacy throughout the lifecourse*. Abingdon: Routledge.

9

USING SELF-STUDY OF PRACTICE TO EXAMINE PEDAGOGIES THAT PROMOTE MEANINGFUL PARTICIPATION

Ciara Griffin and Tim Fletcher

Situating the research: Ciara's story

I grew up on a farm and from an early age was encouraged to be active and healthy. Farming still plays a major part in my everyday life, as does sport. I am an avid sportsperson and have a background in Gaelic football, soccer, handball and rugby. I have been playing rugby for the past eight years, representing at provincial level for over five years and international level for the past year. Coupled with my love for sport, I grew up loving physical education. My experiences in the small country school I attended led to me wanting to become an encouraging and supportive teacher. I studied teaching at university and recently became qualified to teach in Irish primary schools.

Following my graduation, I wanted to complete a master's degree for professional and educational betterment. I am quite an ambitious person and I enjoyed the prospect of pushing myself beyond my comfort zone and learning something new by carrying out research. Prior to completing my master's research, I had very little experience of carrying out academic research. My teaching degree was not research-oriented and I did not have experience of completing a final-year project or thesis.

During my learning at the beginning of my master's degree, what struck me were the reasons why not everyone likes or wants to do physical education. This caused me to think back to my own experiences in school and sport: I always loved participating in physical education and sport. However, I came to a quick conclusion that people participate in physical activities for different reasons such as health, friendship, ambition and many others. What I wanted to learn about were ways to create a physical education learning environment that provided all these motivating factors for children. As a newly qualified teacher it was a complex idea that I viewed timidly at first, but as the research developed I felt I had really found my calling. I had been reading about the challenges of fostering meaningful experiences for learners and decided to carry out research on this topic as it is an area that I felt could be applicable to all areas of education and sport. As a teacher heading out into the professional world, the insights I would gain could be of major benefit to me and hopefully to others.

Background of the research

There have been many compelling arguments made about why teachers or coaches should give priority to fostering meaningful participation in physical education and youth sport (Kretchmar, 2008); however, not so much is known about how teachers and coaches might go about this. Kretchmar (2006) offered some important insights into meaningful movement experiences that promote the habit and persistence seen in lifelong commitment to physical activity participation. He suggested that physical education teachers and coaches should offer experiences that promote: social interaction, challenge, motor competence, fun, and delight. What Ciara wanted to do was to use these ideas to help her make decisions about her planning, teaching, and assessment of the tag rugby unit.

Aims of the research

The main aim of Ciara's research was to develop and articulate pedagogies that support pupils' meaningful participation in primary physical education. To approach the research she would:

- examine her own experiences of implementing strategies, activities and approaches in primary physical education that fostered personally meaningful experiences (generating a teacher's perspective); and
- examine children's experiences of those strategies, activities and approaches (generating learners' perspectives).

The research was carried out in two schools close to Limerick, Ireland. The first school had a strong tradition playing Gaelic Athletic Association (GAA) games (such as hurling, camogie, and Gaelic football). Because of these traditions, none of the 26 children in the grade 4 class Ciara would be working with had experience of tag rugby. Children in the second school were similar to those in the first, with none of the 34 children having played tag rugby before.

A rationale for using self-study of practice methodology

While the research aims seem relatively straightforward, once we situate Ciara in the research process, things become a little more complex because we need to acknowledge the ways her biography colours how she teaches. For example, like most other beginning teachers she might struggle with the unfamiliarity of a new school – meeting new principals, teachers, students, and parents – and coming to terms with her feelings and emotions in that school. In addition to being situated in this research as a new teacher, Ciara and her supervisors also felt that teaching tag rugby through a game-sense or teaching games for understanding (TGfU) approach would be the best way to structure lessons to generate meaningful experiences for students. However, Ciara had limited experiences learning about and being exposed to pedagogical models such as TGfU. This stood in contrast to much of her own learning as a physical education student and elite rugby player, which she suggests could be described as a more traditional, skill-drill-based approach to learning games.

The reasons for considering Ciara's biography and background is because it demonstrates how research into teaching involves much more than simply examining the implementation of lesson plans. Ciara – her *self*, her identities, and her biography – would necessarily be an important part of any data generated.

A reason why Ciara chose not to align her study with the other approaches to practitioner research described in the book was in part due to the crucial role of interactivity embedded in self-study of practice design (LaBoskey, 2004). Ciara could benefit from interacting with a critical friend in the study because of the multiple new challenges she is facing. In addition, she could also benefit from interacting with the students who are learning through the pedagogies she enacts. Further, by engaging in self-study of practice research, Ciara was making a commitment to, and saw the value in, sharing her work with her professional (or discourse) communities so that it might spark debate and help to generate knowledge or a shared understanding of teaching practice.

The research process using self-study of practice methodology

The processes Ciara followed in her research aligned with LaBoskey's (2004) and Samaras's (2010) criteria for quality in self-study of practice research designs. Although these appear as a list, it is worth remembering that most self-study researchers consider these as integrative elements (one feeds off and/or informs the other) rather than a checklist.

1   Self-studies are self-initiated and self-focused

Like many students conducting formal research projects, the line of inquiry Ciara pursued in her research hinged quite a lot on her supervisors' interests, knowledge, and expectations. Déirdre Ní Chróinín and Tim co-supervised Ciara's research project and hers fell somewhere in the middle of the range in terms of Ciara or her supervisors making decisions about her topic. When Ciara enrolled in the master's programme, she was interested in looking at something related to providing positive experiences through games teaching with primary-aged students. Déirdre and Tim had been conducting a longitudinal collaborative self-study on the ways they taught future teachers to provide meaningful experiences for physical education students and so had strong background knowledge and expertise in that area from both theoretical and methodological perspectives. Ciara could adapt her project to fulfil her own interests while building on her supervisors' expertise and previous research. Importantly, engaging in this topic would also provide a solid form of professional learning for Ciara as both a practitioner *and* a researcher.

2 Self-studies are improvement-aimed

The second of LaBoskey's (2004) criteria for quality in self-study research design helps distinguish it from other methodologies that involve reflective practice or inquiry. Because the practitioner has a desire to improve something – be it themselves, their practice, their understanding of pedagogy or learners – it requires them to map out some fairly specific questions to guide the self-study of practice inquiry. Some other forms of practitioner research, such as narrative inquiry or autoethnography, provide space for the practitioner to explore the past inductively to understand or interpret their biography, identity, practice, or something else of interest. Self-study of practice allows for consideration of the past but primarily in the sense of how the past (particularly the self-in-the-past) informs the present or future.

Ciara's topic and research questions laid out specifically the things that she wanted to improve through conducting the research. She had a clear focus on *improving her understanding and enactment of her pedagogy*, particularly as it relates to fostering children's meaningful experiences in physical education. Her own experiences are informed by the lesson plans she develops, the location of the lessons, the interactions she has with children, the ways children interact with and respond to the activities, and so on. An important feature of focusing on improvement is that it acknowledges the doubts, uncertainties, and confusion that many practitioners have about the problematic nature of teaching or coaching practice. Implied in this is an acknowledgment that the processes of self-study required Ciara to be honest about things that did not go well or to plan, or things that she did not understand. The project should not be viewed as a means to self-justification of practices that a practitioner thinks work effectively (Loughran, 2004); it is, however, a way to deeply explore a problem or challenge the practitioner has identified, acknowledge the complexity of professional practice (particularly teaching) and examine possible solutions or aspects for further inquiry.

3 Self-studies are interactive

It is crucial that practitioner researchers who use self-study methodology involve others in some way in the project. Those others could include critical friends or colleagues, students, or texts and their role is to push the practitioner researcher to think in new or different ways about practice. Not only does this carry the potential for transformative thinking about teaching or coaching, it also helps researchers who are involved in formal research (that might be presented or published) to avoid the self-indulgent navel-gazing that early critics of self-study rightly identified.

Following the identification of her research questions, it made sense that Ciara should engage a critical friend, a 'trusted person who asks provocative questions, provides data to be examined through another lens, and offers critique of a person's work as a friend' (Costa & Kallick, 1993, p. 50). Because Ciara was a newly qualified teacher it was important that the critical friend had a knowledge and understanding of some of the issues about (a) being a new teacher, and (b) meaningful experiences in physical education. It was also important that the critical friend be positioned in a way that Ciara was able to speak openly about the challenges she was facing as a teacher without fear of humiliation or consequence. For example, asking a teacher or administrator at one of the schools may have exposed some of the struggles Ciara was having as a new teacher and had implications for future employment.

Tim volunteered to work with Ciara as a critical friend based on the issues mentioned above. He had been involved in several collaborative self-studies prior to this, acting as critical friend to teacher educator colleagues. In addition, he had been involved in an ongoing research project focused on fostering meaningful experiences in physical education and was thus able to focus his questions and feedback on issues central to the research questions. While these experiences were helpful, this was the first time he had been a critical friend to a teacher working in schools. This required him to ask questions and help Ciara consider alternatives in the Irish professional context with which he was not familiar. In addition, he and Ciara had no prior relationship and so they had to establish a personal-professional relationship at the same time as ensuring the critical friendship evolved in ways that supported the research. Tim was therefore required to be open-minded to re-learning about the realities of teaching in schools and how those realities could influence Ciara's research and her interpretation of the results. He was also required to be open-minded about how his personal-professional relationship with Ciara would develop and how this might influence the research process. Therefore, Ciara and Tim had to remain open to learning about and from each other, and to be honest with each other throughout the process.

The second form of interactivity Ciara chose involved students she taught. She chose to conduct the research in two schools so she could get a better sense of the extent to which her teaching and the content of her approach was consistent (or not) with different students who all come from different backgrounds, with different interests, abilities and so on. Researching your own students' experiences of your teaching can pose some ethical issues, particularly related to the power dynamics in any teaching–learning relationship. A lot of children feel an obligation to tell an adult what they think the adult wants to hear rather than their honest opinion, and this has strong and serious consequences for the outcomes and evidence generated by the data and its analysis. Questions about the trustworthiness might be called into question.

As with any formal research (that is, research conducted through a university or other research institution), Ciara would require a full ethical clearance from her university and from the individual school (and maybe even school board or district) before she could officially collect any student data. Because her students were all under the age of 18, this also required her to get informed consent (a form of permission) from the students *and* their parents/guardians. Many teachers in schools collect data from their students to inform their practice – observing and talking to students in class or collecting student work samples. These informal forms of data and data collection do not typically require any approval from research ethics boards and are an essential element of good teaching. The difference in this research is that Ciara was affiliated with the university and not the schools, and was asking students to participate in her research for the purposes of formal analysis and dissemination through various professional channels (such as conferences and in professional magazines or journals). Many school boards or districts employ researchers and have their own research ethics boards, and so if you are thinking about conducting research that goes beyond the typical data collection and analysis involved in doing your job as a teacher, it might be a good idea to run it by someone who has the necessary knowledge of ethics obligations before proceeding too far.

4   Self-studies involve collecting multiple forms of (mostly qualitative) data

There are dozens of data sources that any researcher can choose from when conducting a study but it is important that the research questions or topic guide the types of data to be collected and the methods through which those data are gathered. It is also important that the practitioner researcher provides an audit trail of all of the things they did along the way that helped them arrive at their conclusions at the end of the research project. This helps bolster the trustworthiness of the claims made by the practitioner researcher.

Ciara's research questions provide the best starting place to think about the best data collection methods to use. The first question involves Ciara's experiences of implementing the approach with children and, as with any self-study, there was a need to identify appropriate methods that would allow Ciara to generate the necessary data herself. Rather than just cherry-picking methods from a text book, she wanted to pick the methods that would give her good data showing her insights as well as the challenges, messiness, and complexities involved in teaching.

- *Teacher-generated artefacts.* These are documents that Ciara generated herself. Specifically, she used her unit and lesson plans, reflective journals, and recorded conversations with Tim. When analysed, these artefacts might reveal some of her assumptions about her role as a teacher, her views of students and learning or her interpretations of how tag rugby content could be taught in ways that foster meaningful experiences.
- *Student-generated artefacts.* Data generated by and with the children was an important data source that supported the teacher-generated data Ciara gathered. Student-generated data included verbal (individual and focus group interviews), visual (drawings) and textual (diary entries, stories and poems)

data related to their experiences of pedagogies Ciara used to foster meaningful participation. Below is an example of an acrostic poem a student wrote about her or his tag rugby experience. We have italicised theoretical components of a meaningful experience suggested by Kretchmar (2006):

Tag Rugby is the best
A lot of *fun* we have
Great fun while getting fit

Running around and around
Understanding the rules
Getting *time with my friends*
Bringing new sports to our school
You are the best Ciara

Ciara was able to use this poem to support claims that the children were participating in experiences they deemed meaningful according to the criteria she had identified prior to the research officially beginning (i.e. fun, social interaction, challenge, motor competence, and delight) (Kretchmar, 2006) and that she was trying to enact in her teaching practice. If she had relied solely on self- (or teacher-generated) data, the claims she made in her analysis about her teaching might be less trustworthy.

5 Self-studies are valid if they represent trustworthy accounts and interpretations

At its core, validity reflects the extent to which the researchers are investigating what they are claiming to investigate. As a corollary, a reader of research should ask themselves: Does this research report the findings that the researchers say they are investigating? Is this research credible and believable?

In qualitative research, many scholars of research methodology believe that validity is not the best term because the interpretations about what the qualitative data is revealing are unapologetically subjective. Because qualitative researchers rely so heavily on interpretation, they have a responsibility to convey to the reader that they have not taken liberty with the data to support their own preconceptions and assumptions. Self-study researchers can do this by: being transparent in data collection and analysis procedures; using multiple data sources, each of which provides a unique angle into the lives of the practitioner research participants; sharing evidence of cases that are contrasting or disconfirming, and providing evidence of the ways in which the research has led to a change in the practitioner researcher's beliefs and enactment of practice (Feldman, 2003; LaBoskey, 2004).

For teachers who might share the findings with colleagues in departments or schools or on blogs, or coaches who might share findings with fellow coaches in clubs or on blogs, the findings should be interpreted in ways that their peers can relate to. Encourage the audience to ask themselves: Does what I have just heard resonate with my experiences of teaching or coaching? If the answer is yes, it should indicate that you have offered an honest, transparent, but insightful account of the problem you have set out to explore. The audience also need to hear about the things that didn't work, that remain unresolved, or that were confusing. Hearing those things allows readers to understand all of the elements of a problem so they can judge for themselves the extent to which things you described worked based on the way you have balanced those with things that didn't. An honest account of the research situation tends to be more credible, and therefore more trustworthy. Trustworthy accounts enable a more sophisticated and rigorous development of knowledge of practice to be generated.

Analysing the data

Once the data had been gathered, Ciara had to analyse it. While this is the next logical step in the research process, it is important to think about how the data will be analysed well before it has been gathered. This is because some issues with data gathering can be identified before they cause significant problems in the research process. For example, in analysing self-study data, a practitioner researcher should think about threats to trustworthiness. Recruiting critical friends or non-participant observers in data gathering and analysis can then be established from the outset of the project rather than as an afterthought.

When analysing data, self-study researchers tend to look for things that provide evidence of a shift in thinking or a deepening in understanding about the self-in-practice. Ciara used Bullock and Ritter's (2011) description of such moments as *turning points*. Once Ciara had read through and identified excerpts or instances in the data that she felt represented a turning point, she had to be careful to include all of the relevant data sources that informed the turning point: reflective journals, student work, comments from her critical friend, and so on. Depending on the substance of each turning point, she could choose to represent the turning points standing alone or she could group them according to patterns or themes. Her ultimate decision rested upon where she intended to share her work. For academic presentations and journals, substantive grouping of data tends to be more trustworthy than one-off accounts; however, if she were sharing her findings with departmental colleagues, brief but rich accounts can be just as insightful as the drawing together of several.

A brief summary of the insights gained from using self-study of practice methodology

The following section summarises what Ciara gained from the self-study of practice research process in her own words:

> Self-study of practice supported a systematic investigation into my practice, which allowed for professional learning and the sharing of the understandings

and insights I gained in the process. Engaging in the research to explore pedagogies focused toward meaningful experiences resulted in an improvement of my practice through the use of new approaches, by teaching new topics, and generating and analysing evidence about the effectiveness of this pedagogical approach.

Conducting this self-study research leads me to make some recommendations to people seeking to engage in self-study for the first time. First, it is helpful to choose a critical friend with experience and interests in a similar field as you. Also, ensure your critical friend is both supportive and critical. A reflection template that both parties agree upon can give structure to your reflections but also allow you to clearly track your progress as the research develops. When engaging in self-study I recommend researchers to be open to change – in their assumptions, beliefs, practices, and ways of teaching. Through engaging openly in the self-study process, it allowed me to rethink what teaching physical education means, involves, and looks like to teachers and learners alike. For example, carrying out my research into identifying meaningful pedagogies required me to separate my own experience of sport from my teaching of physical education to others. By coming to better understand the nature of my own sporting experience from the outset I was able to view my teaching with a fresh outlook. Separating my own experience of elite sport gave me the freedom to try new pedagogies in my teaching as I no longer felt the pressure to reflect my own method of sport participation in my teaching.

Second, beginning and experienced practitioners could use self-study as a strong form of professional learning. I found self-study methodology invaluable in supporting my personal and professional development, and it clearly led to the improvement of my practice. This dual purpose of identifying meaningful pedagogies and improving my practice supported Shulman's (1986) belief that good practice requires teachers to have good pedagogical content knowledge and understand what makes the learning of topics easy or difficult for participants. Learning about and understanding children's experiences enabled me to meet the diverse needs of participants in relation to meaningful experiences. As Hamilton and Pinnegar wrote, one of the advantages of using self-study is that it enables us to confidently 'change our practice without waiting for new research from others' (Hamilton and Pinnegar, 2000, p. 238). Throughout the research process I identified problems occurring in my practice and looked for solutions (for example, initially I was overly focusing on the cognitive dimension of learning). As my confidence grew, children acknowledging their own and others' feelings while participating in activities became more rewarding for me rather than focusing on 'how much' they were learning. Reflecting on and analysing the multiple data sources collected in the research supported not only a deeper understanding of my practice but also of the children's experiences of the tag rugby unit.

Prior to this investigation I had no previous experience of carrying out research; formal or otherwise. It was major learning process. For that reason I found LaBoskey's (2004) criteria for quality in self-study design served as a helpful guide. In particular, her criterion of interactivity gave me the space to focus on my self, while also being open to new interpretations of my practice. The collaborative nature of self-study allowed me to shed light on areas of my practice I may have otherwise overlooked as my critical friend provided a different viewpoint on my teaching. It was during discussion with Tim that new ideas about practice were generated and some questions answered. The self-study process enabled me to implement a rigorous inquiry into what has shaped my experiences and my teaching, thus supporting me in improving my practice. In turn, sharing these insights may help others to better understand their own practice, particularly in relation to providing meaningful experiences for children in physical education. From my experience, I support claims that conducting self-study research into one's practice supports academic growth, continuous personal and professional development, knowledge generation, and the enrichment of self-confidence (Lunenberg et al., 2011).

References

Bullock, S. M., & Ritter, J. K. (2011). Exploring the transition into academia through collaborative self-study. *Studying Teacher Education, 7*(2), 171–181.

Costa, A. L., & Kallick, B. (1993). Through the lens of a critical friend. *Educational Leadership, 51*, 49–51.

Feldman, A. (2003). Validity and quality in self-study. *Educational Researcher, 32*(3), 26–28.

Hamilton, M. L., & Pinnegar, S. (2000). On the threshold of a new century: Trustworthiness, integrity, and self-study in teacher education. *Journal of Teacher Education, 51*(3), 234–240.

Kretchmar, R. S. (2006). Ten more reasons for quality physical education. *Journal of Physical Education, Recreation and Dance, 77*(9), 6–9.

Kretchmar, R. S. (2008). The increasing utility of elementary school physical education: A mixed blessing and unique challenge. *The Elementary School Journal, 108*(3), 161–170.

LaBoskey, V. K. (2004). The methodology of teaching and its theoretical underpinnings. In J. J. Loughran, M. L. Hamilton, V. K. LaBoskey, & T. Russell (eds), *International handbook of self-study of teaching and teacher education practices* (pp. 817–869). Dordrecht: Kluwer Academic Press.

Loughran, J. J. (2004). A history and context of self-study of teaching and teacher education practices. In J. J. Loughran, M. L. Hamilton, V. K. LaBoskey, & T. Russell (eds), *International handbook of self-study of teaching and teacher education practices* (pp. 7–39). Dordrecht: Kluwer Academic Press.

Lunenberg, M., Korthagen, F., & Zwart, R. (2011). Self-study research and the development of teacher educators' professional identities. *European Educational Research Journal, 10*(3), 407–420.

Samaras, A. P. (2010). *Self-study teacher research: Improving your practice through collaborative inquiry.* Thousand Oaks, CA: Sage.Shulman, L. S. (1986). Those who understand: Knowledge growth in teaching. *Educational Researcher, 15*(2), 4–14.

PART IV

10

ACKNOWLEDGING BIAS

Introduction

In this chapter we attempted to better understand the affinities and differences between the methodologies in terms of how they position researcher bias. Bias is a slippery word, and is signified differently by different paradigms and individuals. From a post-positivist, quantitative perspective – the dominant paradigm that still drives research in many ways – bias could be seen as any tendency throughout the research process that takes away from the Truth (using capital-T Truth to signify the positivist notion that Truth can be garnered through objective research processes). To work with this definition, you would of course have to believe that there is a singular Truth that lies outside of individual lived experience. This could also be considered a realist perspective. Tied up then in bias, defined this way, are notions of validity, objectivity and certainty.

In contrast, from a qualitative perspective, or critical, pragmatist, constructivist, or relativist perspective, the understanding of bias is quite different. 'Qualitative research is multimethod in focus, involving an interpretive naturalistic approach to its subject matter' (Denzin & Lincoln, 1994, p. 2). Therefore, instead of a focus on validity, there is a turn to trustworthiness. Instead of objectivity there is a turn to subjectivity, instead of certainty, there is a sense of uncertainty within which the Truth becomes relative to the researcher, the context and the researched. It becomes quite easy to see how paradigm wars (Gage, 1989) between positivist/quantitative researchers and interpretive/qualitative researchers have ensued and, in our opinion, continue to fester today.

Given that each of the four methodologies fits into the postmodern era and is qualitative in nature, our conversation around acknowledging bias became focused around gaining a better understanding not only of how we acknowledge bias, but also of the role that bias plays in attempting to create a trustworthy, authentic piece of work that resonates with readers. We began our conversation with the question: 'How do you acknowledge bias in your methodology?' While we meandered through that question we came to wonder about why bias needs to be acknowledged and struggled with how each methodology may take up the term *validity*.

Acknowledging bias

LEE: From reading each other's pieces I really got the sense that when thinking about bias we're not thinking about some abstract phenomenon that might hinder the validity of a research project; the bias is right there. In fact, the relationship between the researcher and the researched creates bias. Objectivity is not what you are after, it is subjective. So then how do we think about validity if we are acknowledging that we are biased?

ASH: I worry about the idea of validity myself; as a term and a concept. In short, I don't know that's a term I would use, or 'we' would use that term in action research. We might use the terms: trustworthy or authentic. You know if we are positioning these methodologies as interpretive, then it can't be the term validity. Is that a methodological consideration that runs across all four studies?

TIM: I know in self-study they talk about validation as a process that is couched within trustworthiness. I think they are terms that mean similar things depending on the paradigm, but then there are preferences for each of us. So, in order to make ourselves understood across the paradigm, having a term or a concept that means something similar will allow others to resonate with it. That's how I see the application of trustworthiness or validity. I prefer trustworthiness. I am not hung up on it being right or wrong, it is just the one I prefer.

DOUG: I would agree with that: trustworthiness rather than validity. And part of that is being true to the methodology you are using. Especially when we are looking at this as practitioner inquiry, trustworthiness comes in the outcome or result. So, if I realise through my autoethnography that I have been sexist, and that I have been treating the females in the class differently than the males, then the trustworthiness comes in what I do about it, as well as the process of the methodology.

TIM: I raised that in my response to this question too Doug. I saw two ways to understand bias. I could think about the bias in my practice. Which is why I thought this was a good question to ask for someone who wanted to use self-study. If self-studies look at the self-in-practice, you can think about how your bias is represented in your practice. But you can also look at how your bias is represented in your research. The subjectivity that you bring to it, the way you analyse and interpret the findings. I could see it working in two ways, but then the challenge becomes: How do you make that coherent throughout both?

DOUG: Yes. I like how you put the aspect in your response about the self and the self-as-researcher – important to acknowledge. Other forms like interpretive inquiry they talk about embracing your subjectivities, by laying them out there because we can't get rid of them. By realising who I am and where I come from, that opens the conversation. And I think that's where autoethnography is like narrative inquiry and self-study in the sense that you are not trying to hide who you are. You are not trying to do some double-blind study to make it valid. You are trying to embrace the fact that you are a part of the study and you are putting it right out there.

ASH: I find that interesting, just returning to my PhD. Guba and Lincoln (2005, p. 205) see validity 'as an irritating construct and one neither easily dismissed or readily configured which leaves with multiple sometimes conflicting mandates in regard to what constitutes rigorous research'. And it's socially and culturally responsive. To me that typifies the work we are doing here.

LEE: I don't think I would use the term valid in narrative inquiry, other than to describe the methodological process that you went through. I think the trustworthiness, as Tim and Doug both described it, comes from being very clear about all the ways in which you may be biased. It's a given that bias is a part of the study. In narrative inquiry we talk about verisimilitude – similar to self-study from what I read – where we really try and collect a variety of field texts in a variety of contextual moments to show you are not just cherry picking moments that show how amazing your study was, the Hollywood story, or how much your practice has changed because of a particular study. Believ-ability, it is part of how you methodologically tell the story. Does it make sense to the reader? So perhaps terms like trustworthiness, authenticity, allow us to talk across methods and sort of show that there are other ways to show a study is valid simply beyond realist Truth.

ASH: When you talk about validity from psychological perspectives, there is population validity, ecological validity, or historical validity. You could follow the same processes but you would not get the same answers in any of these things. I think you can make a statement about validity. The gold standard of scientific research is that external validity refers to the extent to which the results of a study can be generalised to other settings.

DOUG: Verisimilitude, trustworthiness or validity, which one do you use? Because these are all individual methods, they have to do with the person, the person is involved. It's trusting yourself and that you are doing this for a reason that makes sense to you. So, what I mean is if I am an autoethnographer and I go into a study and say: 'You know what? I just want to write a piece of work that shows what an awesome PE teacher I am', then I am not being trustworthy. I am not being true to myself. But if I am actually being true to myself I am going to go find that team contract that I made everyone sign, and I am going to dig in to how sexist it actually was. That is being true to myself and the research. And I think that is an important part of each of these methodologies.

LEE: Important point. I think we are straddling those borderland research spaces that bump with epistemological beliefs about what counts and what does not count. So in many methods personal justification isn't even part of the conversation. In fact, a personal justification would be seen as subjective and would perhaps increase the bias involved in a study.

On reflection, it is clear from our discussion that we were working through the nuances of each methodology as we struggled with acknowledging bias. We certainly saw affinities as we looked across the methodologies. It became clear that each of us struggled with the dominant meaning of validity. Like other qualitative researchers, the use of words such as authenticity, verisimilitude, and trustworthiness provide each of us with tools to illustrate the merit of our work outside of the quantitative structures that poorly align with our research (Given & Saumure, 2008). For each of us it seems that the transparency of conscious bias is an important part of research that is trustworthy. Therefore, a clear message to the reader about how you will account for bias becomes an important aspect of each methodology.

This focus on transparency moves beyond simply reflecting on our own individual bias as researchers, to how we are situated within the environments within which we teach and research. For example, identifying yourself as privileged within a social-system may construe a bias that someone who is underprivileged may not have. All four of us come from privileged positions within the social systems we are part of: we are white, middle-class, heterosexual males and recognise that these characteristics and the experiences we have been afforded lead us to have certain biases and assumptions that others from different backgrounds with different experiences may not have. Therefore, self-reflection and inquiry, along with inquiry into how the researcher or teacher is situated socially, also seems to be an important aspect of each method when thinking about acknowledging bias.

While acknowledging bias by explicitly naming it is important, it also seemed that a rigorous accounting of the entire research process from study design to methodological selection to data collection to analysis and to final research texts was seen by each of us as being important. Even if we are constantly thinking about our biases, we can never really identify all of the ways in which our biases may impact our practice or research. It seems that a rigorous account of the process at least allows the reader to better understand how our biases played a role in each of the decisions made.

As our conversation progressed we continued to discuss ways of acknowledging bias but the discussion took a nuanced shift as we began to think about what acknowledging bias does. What does acknowledging bias do for us as teachers/coaches and as researchers? What effect might acknowledging bias have on the reader?

TIM: To go back to verisimilitude, my understanding is it means to have research ring true to a reader. And if we want things to ring true, then laying those things on the line is important so that the reader can walk a mile in our shoes so to speak. If they really want to engage with the research, then we have a responsibility to discuss our biases in a lot of detail and so on and so forth. I was also thinking about what validity means or what it represents. To boil it down to a layperson's terms, it's about strength, the strength of the research. And for our research to be read as being strong we need to have confirming interpretations and we need to bounce that off the disconfirming pieces. If it is just sunshine and lollipops it does not resonate with the realities of the reader and their experience as a practitioner.

DOUG: I like the idea of strength. Authentic, I wrote that down . . . we need to be authentic to ourselves, to our methodology, to the story we are telling and to the action we want to pursue. Back to bias, all of these methods are inherently biased because these are all studies of ourselves. Like Tim said, people can see themselves in our shoes. In the published autobiographical narrative inquiry I did with Lee, when I talk to my students about that work, although they did not live my stories, they see elements of that authenticity in their own stories and we can connect in those ways.

LEE: What Doug is speaking to there, I think, is the transactional nature of narrative inquiry. Even though the narrative, story, experience is not necessarily yours, if it's authentic, trustworthy, it can resonate for others in different contexts.

ASH: And that kind of returns to the narrative conception of stories to live by. Around the expectations behind what is normal. What is normative in teaching, in this case PE teaching? Some of it is that process of you know, it's the jarring, the bumping against the dominant stories, and it's those things in narrative that sort of allow authenticity. From an action research stand point, as Elliot (1991) suggested, when research is actioned it moves from a passive reproduction. Ideas and intent move us to an active production of meaning. Consequently, we acknowledge our bias as an awakening, the manifestation of human powers. So it's not about passively deciding that something is correct in my background, like curriculum, but about a process of meaning-making and being in action with that meaning. But also acknowledging that we have unconscious bias, we see that in what we teach and what becomes the null curriculum.

TIM: From a self-study perspective, as Loughran (2007) says, self-study can't be seen as a route to self-justification. I think that resonates with what both Ash and Lee had mentioned. So I see a lot of resonance across the four methodologies but at the same time see some distinctions between how each would approach it.

LEE: But the end goal is not necessarily to shape practice. What happens when you have researchers in classrooms, in relationship, alongside students and teachers? It just happens that from that relationship, things will change. And you know there is a lot of humbleness that comes with each of these methodologies, you are not the expert here. You don't have all of the knowledge. Being humble is not that easy to do in these academic places. So it can sometimes be a really tough place to be.

TIM: Maybe that's what sort of signifies practitioner research, and perhaps these four methodologies in some way. If you are going to engage in this work it's not to tell the world how good you are. It's to show how much you don't know. But also to show how you can improve.

ASH: Mockler and Groundwater-Smith (2009) ask the practitioner researcher, and those who support him or her, to move beyond celebration and see the realities of practice. Cook (2009) asks us to be conscious of the messy turn, and I've asked readers to be aware of not just the steps but also the processes in action research. In doing so teachers and coaches become experts. Consequently, I am going to disagree with Lee, and say that teachers and coaches are expert. I think they are expert in their own context and expert at the point of implementation.

LEE: I agree with that Ash. In fact, that is really where Jean Clandinin's work came from in some ways I think. From working in schools as a researcher and having other researchers talk about how little knowledge teachers had. And being a person who was working with teachers, she was sort of like, well actually teachers have a lot of knowledge, we just don't really ask them. So I think that is really at the heart of what we are doing. I was just thinking about Tinning's (2002) notion of modest pedagogy, which is kind of a rebuttal to critical theories that have sort of driven people to critically analysing social structures without actually looking into how you are situated within those larger social structures. So this humble pedagogy sort of asks us to show some humility as we think about these complex issues. And I think that humbleness, and transparency, resonates with the teacher, the researcher and perhaps the reader.

ASH: Well okay, I have a question for you three. Is action research the worst at acknowledging bias because it does not start from self? Well I think the others (narrative inquiry, autoethnography, and self-study) all acknowledge self first as opposed to last . . . I think it is a methodological decision to not begin with biases. It comes at a later point with action research, but it is not the starting point?

DOUG: I think that bias comes in any time. Whether you are studying yourself or others, it is still going to come in . . . Autoethnography, I think, starts there. I think the starting point is culture. It is acknowledged early. It starts with the self, but really sort of the self within that culture

LEE: Interesting, I don't know that the beginning of a narrative inquiry is strictly about acknowledging your biases. It may become a part of it, especially when you lay your own stories alongside others' stories. But also, when you immediately acknowledge bias, I think it can really reduce you down to sort of demographic markers. I am a white male, tall, play sports. Immediately you have a notion of who I am, in a reduced way. But I think in narrative inquiry you really want to get beyond the sociocultural to start. You want to really think about your experiences, how you make sense of them over time, in places, and then perhaps get to the sociocultural aspects. I think maybe that is one of the differences between narrative inquiry and autoethnography.

DOUG: I would agree with you, Lee. I think we have to be careful how we acknowledge bias. I may use the term subjectivities which sort of puts less of a negative spin on it. It's more about recognising where I come from, more of acknowledging it and putting it out there than saying this defines me.

LEE: Because there is a multiplicity of stories. You can't be reduced to gender, race, socio-economic status, etc. Even though it happens all of the time. From an interpretivist framework, we are sort of saying there are multiple realities, it's not one truth or one story, one way to intervene to fix it. It's more like there are multiple ways to understand from a variety of perspectives which include our own biases and subjectivities.

There are a variety of ways to take up the field texts from our conversation, but perhaps the most important for us is how the researcher is situated within the research and alongside the practitioner. In the search for 'Truth', oftentimes any type of relationship would be seen as fostering a potential subjective research bias (Schaefer, Lessard, Panko & Pulsfut, 2014); however, with the methodologies discussed in this book it is quite clear that Truth is not what we are after. Interestingly, it is the explicit research biases made visible during the research process that may indeed help a piece of work to be perceived as trustworthy.

From a research perspective trustworthiness may be perceived as transparency into the research process; however, to a practitioner reading the research it would be better described as an account that resonates with their experiences working in the field.

Practitioners are constantly bombarded with information, policy, curriculum and mandates from the conduit (Clandinin & Connelly, 1995); oftentimes the perception, from teachers, is that those passing on the orders are not actually teachers. Being in relationship with practitioners as we take up research questions provides the messiness, contexts and uncertainty that comes with being a teacher or researcher in complex knowledge landscapes. Making this messiness transparent, as opposed to reducing it, may be one reason that each of these methodologies resonates with practitioners.

Conclusion

In this chapter we took up two questions: (1) How does each of the methodologies discussed in this book acknowledge bias? (2) What comes from acknowledging this bias in regard to trustworthiness? In attempting to answer these questions we attempted to show not only the collateral impact of bias, but also how researchers using differing paradigms and methodologies may think about bias. Seeing that bias is often linked to validity in quantitative methods, we also wanted to show the importance of bias when using the four qualitative methodologies illustrated in this book.

There are some key points that emerged as we thought about bias with each of the methodological lenses:

- The term validity often attached to bias can be thought about in the aforementioned methods as authenticity, trustworthiness, authenticity and verisimilitude.

- Trustworthiness stems from the researcher's ability to situate themselves within the research, laying out the researcher's biases and assumptions, providing transparency to the research process.
- While each methodology acknowledges bias, when and how bias is taken up differs. This speaks to how the self is situated differently in each methodology.
- While relationships in research may be seen as creating bias, these relationships also provide a contextual messiness that resonates with practitioners' experiences of teaching.

Given the inductive nature of this chapter, we are in no way insinuating that these are hard and fast rules that must be adhered to in regard to acknowledging bias. They are simply starting points for those who may engage with these methodologies to begin thinking about how bias shapes not only their research decisions, but also in many ways who the research may be for.

References

Clandinin, D.J., & Connelly, M.F. (1995). *Teachers' professional knowledge landscapes*. New York: Teachers College Press.

Cook, T. (2009). The purpose of mess in action research: Building rigour though a messy turn. *Educational Action Research, 17*(2): 277–291.

Denzin, N.K., & Lincoln, Y.S. (1994). *Handbook of qualitative research*. Thousand Oaks, CA: Sage.

Elliott, J. (1991). *Action research for educational change*. Milton Keynes: Open University Press.

Given, L.M., & Saumure, K. (2008). Trustworthiness. In L.M. Givens (ed.), *The Sage encyclopedia of qualitative inquiry, vol. 2* (pp. 895–896). Thousand Oaks, CA: Sage.

Guba, E.G., & Lincoln, Y.S. (2005). Paradigmatic controversies, contradictions, and emerging confluences. In N.K. Denzin & Y.S. Lincoln (eds), *The Sage Handbook of Qualitative Research* (3rd edition, pp. 191–215). Thousand Oaks, CA: Sage.

Loughran, J. (2007). Researching teacher education practices: Responding to the challenges, demands, and expectations of self-study. *Journal of Teacher Education, 58*(1), 12–20.

Mockler, N. & Groundwater-Smith, S. (2009). Seeking for unwelcome truths: Action learning beyond celebration. Paper presented to the Pedagogy in Practice Annual Conference, Newcastle, New South Wales, Australia, 21–22 July.

Schaefer, L., Lessard, S., Panko, S., & Polsfut, N. (2014). The temporal turn to narrative inquiry: Bumping places and beyond. In M. Baguley, A. Jasman, & Y. Findlay (eds), *Meanings For In and Of Education Research* (pp. 17–29). New York: Routledge.

Tinning, R. (2002). Toward a 'modest pedagogy': Reflections on the problematics of critical pedagogy. *Quest, 54*(3), 224–240.

11

ETHICAL RESPONSIBILITIES OF BEING A PRACTITIONER RESEARCHER

Introduction

Kuhse and Singer (1998, p. 4) define ethical research as, 'an involvement in a caring, compassionate approach toward understanding what it means to be human and what it means to act morally'. Therefore, an ethical approach to research (and practice) can be (simply) summed up as, 'Do no harm'. The realities of ethics for practitioner researchers are rather more complex, as we quickly uncovered in our dialogue around the construction of this chapter. Traditionally, and maybe surprisingly, research actually has a bit of a shady ethical history. For example, consider the nature of vocabulary such as 'subject' and 'control'. Institutional concerns about ethics and participant rights arose from infamous research studies such as the Tuskegee syphilis experiments, Nazi human experimentation, and others. As an example, the Tuskegee experiments involved the United States Public Health Service tracking the natural progression of syphilis by deceiving rural African American males. Among many of the ethical concerns of this research, the US Public Health Service informed research participants they had been treated for syphilis when in fact they had not (CDC, 2015). This serves as one example of the potentially severe physical, social, and emotional effects research can have on participants. It also serves to emphasise the responsibility researchers have – regardless of the focus of the study – in respecting and protecting the human rights of research participants.

Qualitative and practitioner methodologies are also not immune to ethical issues. For example, according to Holman Jones, Adams and Ellis (2013), ethical (and political) concerns were one of four interrelated trends that led to the emergence of autoethnography. As well, Samaras's (2010) self-study book for teacher–researchers dedicates a whole chapter to ethical considerations, highlighting the importance of thinking and acting ethically while conducting practitioner research.

The key question for this chapter is: 'What are the ethical responsibilities of being a practitioner researcher?' Drawing on each of the four methodologies and using a process of discussion, debate, writing and re-writing between the four co-authors, we have examined the varying and similar approaches from each of the methodologies addressed in the book. As we talked and wrote, the following four key themes were generated:

- formal and informal ethical considerations;
- relational ethics (or the ethics of relationships);
- consent, confidentiality and transparency; and
- purpose and audience.

To catalyse our discussion of this practitioner researcher dilemma, we began by writing down some key points and vignettes based on our own experiences and research. The following excerpts from our initial reflections show clearly how the framing of ethical research as a formal process provided a starting point for our conversations:

- *Self-study of practice:* Some self-studies (i.e. those using personal data only) may not require official approval from a research ethics board. However, with any form of practitioner research that uses the perspectives of the learners (students, players) comes an obligation to not only be ethical on a surface level but also to be ethical on an official level. It may be that there are some people who like self-study as a methodology because they feel they do not need to obtain 'formal' approval to conduct publishable research. However, this masks the need for any practitioner researcher to think carefully about how they design self-study research (for example, how will interactivity be included? Or what forms of data will be generated?) and address their research questions in a rigorous way.
- *Narrative inquiry:* Clandinin and Connelly (2000) realised early on in the creation of narrative inquiry that they needed to think about ethics as much more than a terminal process completed at the university before a study begins. In this way the ethical process is imbued in the entire research study from negotiating a research space to co-composing a final research text and must take into account a deeper understanding of what it means to live in relation in ethical ways (Connelly & Clandinin, 2006).
- *Action research:* In their book on ethical approaches to practitioner research, Groundwater-Smith and Campbell (2007, p. 172) asked 'how can we best conduct ourselves in ways that do justice to our practice and our profession?' Throughout this edited monograph different authors considered issues like participation and representation, thoughts and habits, relationships, fairness and, inevitably, power. The danger, of course, is we get so caught up in an

ethical quagmire of our own making that we fail to give the space and time to considering the ethics involved. Just because we can do something doesn't mean we should. Equally, just because something is difficult we shouldn't not do it. Instead, and as Elliott (1991) argues, we need to realise our ethical obligations. This is where, for me, the cycle of plan, think, act, evaluate, reflect is so important. At each stage that obligation to ethical action is vital. We have an obligation to teach to the best of our ability and action research has the potential to help us to see that.

- *Autoethnography:* The cultural aspect of autoethnography requires an extremely ethical approach – especially where culture includes 'others'. For example, in a school environment, your colleagues are part of the culture. Care must be taken, regardless of the public or private nature of the work, to not cause harm. In this manner, we could look at ethics in two ways: policy and practice. Institutional researchers have to go through a formal ethics process – a policy. As well, it is hoped that we also act ethically in all we do with our work – a practice. A teacher or coach using autoethnography may not be required to go through a formal ethical policy, but their practice should certainly be ethical.

Formal and/or informal?

As we began our conversation based on the above reflections, the very first theme we discussed was that of informal versus formal ethical considerations.

TIM: With our positions at a university and our professional obligations, we sort of have it ingrained in our approaches to do things ethically, on a formal or informal level. However, for the readers of this book it is important to be able to tap into what ethics means from their position as a teacher or a coach in a local community. My assumption is that most of the ethics they will be concerned with is of an informal nature. And so, what does that mean? What considerations might they have to take then in being an ethical researcher of their practice in order to allow them to arrive at understandings that make sense to them and potentially to their communities that they are going to be sharing that with?

LEE: I think that that wording of formal/informal is a little bit problematic for me. I think that for each of our research methods there is so much engagement with either a practitioner or participant over an extended period of time that you know in some ways it could become a developmental process for both. So one of the things that I think we need to be mindful of, from a narrative inquiry perspective, is creating ethical rigour within what we are doing so that we are constantly mindful of how complex our ethical commitments really are.

DOUG: Lee, I agree there are limits to the terms formal and informal. Obviously we have some formal processes to go through at a university that don't necessarily exist in the practitioner's world. However, we do need to think about the ramifications of our work. You know, if it's never going to be shared outside of yourself and your own work that's one thing, but even sharing it in a conversation, the last thing we want you to do is throw your colleagues under the bus or really slam some people.

In discussing some research he had conducted in the past, Ash referred to some ethical issues that arose.

ASH: It started to be: 'Well, there isn't one way of interpreting . . .', 'It's a narrow view, it's my view, it's based on my history and the way I perceive things . . .'. And that might be disingenuous to the other people in that site, while I can't speak for them. I can't do that. I need to acknowledge there is more than one side to a story and what I am telling you is my perspective. I think there is an ethical consideration there in terms of how you position yourself, whether it's yourself or whether it's your narrative or whether it's your autobiography or autoethnography, it's how you position yourself.

DOUG: . . . The first thing I wrote down [about this dilemma] is that teaching or coaching, it is research. All the time. It is. So I think to me it's almost, there's ethics as practice and there's ethics as policy and you know, we should all have ethical practice whether or not there is a policy that 'makes us'. It's really about the change that's going on.

TIM: And so, again, how we think of ethics, is that going to be practical and applicable and appropriate for the types of ethical considerations that readers need to be thinking of? I am sort of thinking of it as Ethics (big E ethics) for the type that we need to do in order to get things published or funded or what have you. And ethics (little e ethics), which is being conscious of the rights of your participants or your students or the people that you're working with so they have the right to feel that they are not being coerced into saying or doing something that they don't want to, they are feeling like they can opt out of certain things if they want to.

The position of most practitioner researchers who we assume will be reading this book is that of teacher or coach, which suggests that the work involves teaching/learning. In these types of relationships, there are inherent issues of power. Issues of power are also issues of ethics.

Relational ethics

As has been noted, discussions about ethical research invariably lead to thinking about relationships. The concept of *relational ethics* (Bergum & Dossetor, 2005) includes four basic elements that can be applied to practitioner research:

1   *Mutual respect*: parties in a relationship show regard for each other's feelings, desires, interests, knowledge, or rights. People are unconditionally accepted,

recognised, and acknowledged, and are not treated or made to feel as if they were the same.

2   *Relational engagement*: community connections are a requirement to be attentive to both self and others.

3   *Embodiment*: '. . . expresses recognition that people live in a specific historical and social contexts as thinking, feeling, full-bodied, and passionate human beings' (ibid., p. 137).

4   *Creating environment*: the relational space for ethical action, which is created in each action and in each decision enabling freedom and choice to empower individuals.

Like relationships, ethical research can be – and often is – messy and complex, as we discovered in our conversation.

LEE: . . . There are all these more complex questions (i.e. What happens when the study is over? Do you still keep in touch?) that become *the ethics of relationships as opposed to just the ethics of research*.

DOUG: I read about friendship as method (Tillman-Healy, cited in Adams et al., 2015) which involves asking researchers to approach their relationship with their participants as they would a friendship. So prioritising the relationship, making time, not making inappropriate demands, nurturing the relationship, addressing conflicts, acknowledging issues of confidentiality and loyalty in ways that meet the demands of friendship and research. And then maintaining the relationship after it's complete. Even our formal ethics processes are changing slowly to acknowledge this.

ASH: When I look at ethics, one of the things I tend to point out to practitioner researchers is the 'boy scouts' promise'. I promise to do my best. To do my duty: 'I am going to act in the best way I possibly can. I think that's something good'. There's an interesting piece by Zeni (2009, p. 255), where she says, 'Gradually I realise that action research calls into question the ethical norms that guide the academic modes of inquiry both qualitative and quantitative. The norms of qualitative inquiry have defined the ethical researcher as an outsider; any personal involvement with the people or engagement with the events in a research setting is considered biased.' If research protocol positions me as inherently biased, then how can I act ethically?

TIM: Even though we acknowledge our bias and the positions of power we might be in in relation to student, I think you still act ethically in terms of respecting the rights of participants. They have the right to anonymity, to confidentiality, to withdraw from research without punishment or adverse consequences and those sorts of things. It goes back to our points about big E and little e ethics. The point is that participants need to feel that their voices will be heard in the process and to do that, they need to trust who they are working with.

Consent, confidentiality and transparency

> . . . the ethical advancement of practitioner research relies on the alignment of a
> number of different ethical frames. Those of consent, confidentiality, and transparency.
>
> (Mockler, 2007, p. 88)

These three concepts are often considered to be the foundations of ethical research.
Consent (informed consent) refers to the act of a participant giving permission for
research to take place, be analysed and shared. Confidentiality means that participants have a right to be protected, especially when sharing sensitive information or
personal experiences. Transparency means that there are no 'tricks' or deception –
what you see is what you get. Regardless of where the research falls on the ethical
policy–practice continuum, we felt that consent, confidentiality and transparency
should be always be ensured.

TIM: I think that regardless of what level you're doing research at, even where
there are no official expectations for ethics, it is important that there are some
benchmarks or standards for what you're doing because that's what allows you
to make claims that are grounded in something. If we want to make claims that
have any weight behind them we typically have to follow an ethical process.

ASH: I think the key about ethics is that it's about consent and assent. That's a key
ingredient. I mean, one of the reasons we have ethical procedures is because
people need to give explicit permission to be involved in these things. We
come back to the moral imperative or the ethical imperative of a teacher/
coach, which is to work at the best of their ability to improve their practice –
that in itself becomes ethical.

TIM: The practitioner researcher has some responsibilities if they are acting ethically to be transparent. Such as, 'Hey folks, what you're telling me, I am going
to use that to shape the decisions that I am going to make as your teacher or
coach and help my thinking in the future. I want you to know that what you
tell me, can influence what happens in the future.'

ASH: I think there are different ethical frames around what practitioner researchers
do and what practitioner research is. Some of it is personal, it is informing
practice, but I think ethics of consent is very important just like confidentiality
and transparency.

DOUG: Let's say I am doing some work with my grade 4 students and I've got one
that I am really struggling with. It wouldn't necessarily be ethical for me to
talk with you, Tim, and say this student is driving me nuts. But, when I am
teaching grade 4 and another teacher has my same kids for another subject, it
is ethical to talk about those kids because the goal is to help them. Whereas in
my own research, or in even sharing across disciplines, perhaps I can't do that
because of confidentiality.

LEE: I think there's a reflective wakefulness to ethics that gets lost when we talk
about informed consent and anonymity and those things. And there's no

question that those are institutional ethics and this is a practitioner research book but I think at the end of the day if you have a wakefulness that's more reflective than 'Oh, is this anonymous or not anonymous?' Getting to that relational ethics piece around 'Am I being a good human being?' For me that can transcend the bounds of researcher or practitioner, etc.

Purpose and audience

After establishing the importance, context and nuance of consent, confidentiality and transparency, we inevitably ended up in conversations around the purpose of the research and the audience it is intended for. Ethical considerations must reflect both why the research is being done and with whom (or in what form) the results will be shared.

DOUG: There is a big ethical distinction between audiences and purposes. For example, Lee, if I use your work with Growing Young Movers (see Chapter 7), you're using that data all of the time to improve the programme. You're using that data when you and your colleagues are talking together, when you're planning for the next session. You're using it all the time, as Ash mentioned, to change your practice, to make sure you're being the best teacher or the best programme adviser or the best coach that you can be. However, if I am looking to publish something, that is a different set of standards.

TIM: In thinking about who I assume will be or make up a large part of the audience to this book, I don't think publishing is even on the radar. And so again, how we think of ethics – is that going to be practical and applicable and appropriate for the types of ethical considerations that they need to be thinking of?

ASH: Good point. However, publishing for us is peer-reviewed articles. Publishing for a teacher or coach may be a blog. That's still a published engine, it's still using those narratives and therefore, is it ethical? A lot of people we work with are practitioner researchers who are doing undergraduate or postgraduate study and they are publishing. They might not be publishing to the world but they are publishing for a qualification so I think that whole notion of publication needs to be challenged to make it applicable to those fields.

TIM: So, given that practitioner researchers are likely to disseminate their work through social media or whatever, I think that highlights even further the need to conduct practitioner research in an ethical way and to hold themselves to very high standards.

DOUG: An important piece is to get to that point of constantly thinking about how to frame yourself, how to frame your practitioner inquiry ethically, regardless of how it's shared.

TIM: Or even at a school council meeting where there are parents and teachers talking about the latest things going on. That needs to be considered even though there might only be 10 people in the audience.

LEE: I think we still need to tailor this towards people that are going to be publishing data beyond peer review, larger than the classroom or school or parent council. You know I don't think we have ethical protocols for blogs, we don't right? I mean articles that are published in (some journals) don't ask unless it's peer-reviewed what the ethical process was of collecting that data. I would really like there to be a critical, reflective, thoughtful wakefulness to ethical considerations.

ASH: I think a lot of these things, such as social media, are about ethics. It's about being a decent human being and it's about acknowledging that piece first and foremost, it's not about sensationalising it, it's not about taking our own opportunities as best we can; it's about our own ethical piece and sometimes it's a grey area.

DOUG: A blanket type, formalised ethics process for practitioner researchers – that's not our focus. Our point is to have the discussion like we are having and to recognise that ethics is complex. I like your use of wakefulness, Lee. Ash, your idea of 'this is what it means to be a good human'. So that no matter how you're doing this work or no matter how you're choosing to disseminate or share it, you are concerned about the ethical implications of what's going on.

TIM: So these are really serious considerations that a practitioner researcher has to make. This is not just a knee-jerk reaction that they need to make and think 'Oh it'll be fine'. So yes, this is way more complex than I think I was aware of at the start of the conversation and there are a lot of things people undertaking this type of work need to think about – the implications are massive.

LEE: A caveat: 'Within this chapter what we are trying to look at are the nuances between these four methodologies and how questions, concerns or dilemmas come up as we're thinking about ethics'. So for Doug, thinking about the friendship piece and narrative inquiry, what are the implications for negotiating your way into a research space? In self-study, what are the ethics of a critical friend researcher? Then with Ash, what are the ethical implications of being a teacher–researcher in the school? Hopefully this chapter gets you to go read the handbook on self-study, etc. Or consult your ethics board for your district. Or whatever you need to do to be certain you are acting ethically!

DOUG: So the purpose of ethics is to act as a proper human being, therefore we want the people reading this book to just think about and question their own practices as a human being doing research. Whether it be autoethnography, self-study, narrative inquiry, or action research – be in relationship and be an ethical person. And if in doubt, ask. If you're not sure go to your district. If you're uncertain, talk to your principal, the director of the sports club, etc. about what you're thinking of doing and where you're thinking of publishing it.

For practitioners who are interested in conducting research without an aim of sharing publicly (in journals or on blogs), there is still a need to act ethically, even though formal ethics board approval may not be necessary. Considerations include:

- How will I obtain informed consent?
- How will I anonymise responses if necessary?
- Have I been transparent about the purpose(s) for my work and the audience(s) it will be shared with?
- How will I manage any power dynamic so that participants (or self) are being honest in responses and therefore providing trustworthy data?

In the Part III chapters, you have been given snapshots of how each of the authors has incorporated ethical research principles in their work with coaches and teachers. Above all, these examples serve as a reminder of the diversity of ethical considerations and responsibilities.

Conclusion

As we have seen, ethical considerations (and conversations!) are messy, grey and totally fundamental to all types of practitioner research regardless of purpose, audience or locus. Just 'doing no harm' is really not enough. Thoughtful consideration must be given to consent, confidentiality and transparency at all stages of the research process. Practitioner researchers must be aware of both informal and formal ethics protocols – Ethics and ethics – taking steps to ensure care for participants, researchers and audiences alike. *Friendship as method* (Tillman-Healy, cited in Adams et al., 2015) may be a valuable way for us to conclude this discussion. What this philosophy of ethics comes down to is relationships and treating those we are researching with as friends. If your relationship with participants is seen as a friendship you will:

- prioritise them – not make unrealistic demands and be there when needed;
- nurture the relationship over time;
- handle potential conflicts expeditiously and explicitly;
- meet the needs of both research and friendship when dealing with issues of consent, confidentiality and transparency; and
- maintain the relationship after the research part is over.

References

Adams, T., Holman Jones, S., & Ellis, C. (2015). *Autoethnography: Understanding qualitative research*. New York: Oxford University Press.

Bergum, V., & Dossetor, J. (2005). *Relational ethics: The full meaning of respect*. Hagerstown, MD: University Publishing Group.

CDC. (2015). US public health service syphilis study at Tuskegee. Retrieved from www. cdc.gov/tuskegee/index.html.

Clandinin, D.J., & Connelly, F. M. (2000). *Narrative inquiry: Experience and story in qualitative research*. San Francisco, CA: Jossey-Bass.

Connelly, F.M., & Clandinin, D.J. (2006). Narrative inquiry. In J. Green, G. Camilli & P. Elmore (eds), *Handbook of complementary methods in education research* (pp. 375–385). Mahwah, NJ: Lawrence Erlbaum.

Elliott, J. (1991). A model of professionalism and its implications for teacher education. *British Educational Research Journal, 17*(4), 309–318.

Groundwater-Smith, S., & Campbell, A. (2007). Concluding reflections: New challenges for ethical inquiry in the context of a changing world. In A. Campbell & S. Groundwater-Smith (eds), *An ethical approach to practitioner research* (pp. 172–180) London: Routledge.

Holman Jones, S., Adams, T., & Ellis, C. (Eds.). (2016). *Handbook of autoethnography.* New York: Routledge.

Kuhse H., & Singer P. (Eds.). (1998). *A companion to bioethics.* Oxford: Blackwell.

Mockler, N. (2007). Ethics in practitioner research: Dilemmas from the field. In A. Campbell & S. Groundwater-Smith (eds). *An ethical approach to practitioner research* (pp. 88–98) London: Routledge.

Samaras, A. P. (2010). *Self-study teacher research: Improving your practice through collaborative inquiry.* Thousand Oaks, CA: Sage.

Zeni, J. (2009). Ethics and the 'personal' in action research. In S. Noffke & B. Somekh (eds). *The Sage handbook of educational action research* (pp 254–266). London: Sage.

12

ALIGNING BELIEFS AND ACTIONS

Aligning professional beliefs and actions: a worthy investigation?

In the very act of problematising the similarities and differences between professional beliefs and actions, we quickly realised that it represented an interesting and useful phenomenon to explore through practitioner research. We agreed it was something that could be undertaken by a practitioner researcher using any of the four methodologies presented in this book. That is, a practitioner researcher could consider the ways in which, through their practice, their beliefs and actions align using action research, narrative inquiry, autoethnography, or self-study of practice. In our discussion it became clear, however, that each approach would require the practitioner researcher to prioritise different things within their inquiry, and go about the processes of conducting practitioner research in a slightly different way using each methodology.

Our conversation began by considering the role of beliefs and actions in helping a practitioner researcher identify a starting point for their inquiry. This proved an important place to begin because we understood that the starting point in the practitioner research process ultimately shapes the design and outcomes of the investigation. The conversation then led into thinking about the temporal focus (i.e. the attention an individual affords to their consideration of past, present, and future) that each methodology privileges, and concluded with a consideration of who dictates the framing of the inquiry: the practitioner researcher or an external, governing authority (such as a school board)?

Each methodology acknowledges beliefs and actions

LEE: When I was thinking about [how you incorporate beliefs and actions] . . . it really depends on the methodology as to where you start. I guess with narrative inquiry, part of it is that you need to first understand where your beliefs and values come from and how your stories to live by – or your identities or your subjectivities or however you conceptualise that – how that affects and shapes who you are as a practitioner and what you believe. So I guess as part of the research process . . . you need to engage in the early beginnings, the temporal nature of your experience. Create time-lines and annals and see why you have these beliefs and values at this [par-ticular] point in time, and decide: Is this something that you really need or want to implement into your practice? So that is the first piece. That might be completely different in action research. I was thinking as I was looking at the issue the other day . . . maybe the main thing is to determine how the question you are starting with is [embedded] in your beliefs, and that is where you start.

ASH: I think necessarily with action research, there must be an action and you have to research that action. I wondered whether, in narrative inquiry or in autoethnography, there must be an action? Or whether, through the focus on the self, whether it is just acknowledging beliefs and not an action? In self-study of practice, practice (to me) is an action. So practice is something that you do . . . So with some of these methodologies, I wonder if words speak louder than actions [or if beliefs matter more than actions]? Does that make sense?

TIM: I always try to distinguish self-study from action research and narrative inquiry as having an emphasis on self while also having an emphasis on practice. You can't do one without the other. I have a feeling, from a layperson's perspective I suppose, that action research has the action (or practice) but not necessarily the beliefs. I think it can but it doesn't have to. And yes, narrative inquiry and autoethnography have the beliefs but not necessarily the action. But in self-study of practice, you have to have both – you are always thinking about the self-in-practice.

ASH: But . . . I don't think you can have an action research study that doesn't have that notion of belief. As I asked in [our initial dialogue]: What do you want to action and why do you want to action it? And how will you know what impact those actions have? And ethically, in teaching we must do what we believe [is best] for our students. This may involve positioning practitio-ner research as a hunch that something will work, but how will we know it will work? If it doesn't work, so to speak, does that make it a bad idea or just something that needs to be actioned with more consideration or in the longer term?

DOUG: If I look at [this issue] from an autoethnographic perspective and con-sider actions and beliefs, ethnography is inherently a study of culture but really the way you study culture is to be a part of it and look at it histori-cally. You are looking back at things: critical incidents, observations, stories, documents. So to me, when you study your actions, you look at your beliefs generated in the past and try to figure out if [and how] you put them in action. And so it is examining the past to impact the future. That's how I see how you could use autoethnography to deal with this issue. Say, if you believe that girls should have the same opportunities in sport and physical education as boys, let's look back autoethnographically and see if those beliefs were translated in action in the past. If they were, great! But how do you keep it going? If they weren't, why? Why weren't they translated and how could you shift that?

LEE: One of the interesting things is that ethnography's history is based in anthropology, where people used to go and sit in and observe another culture. But [the researcher] was always an outsider. Whereas with autoethnography, there is a turn: you have to 'self-face'. So I think we've found some pretty significant differences here. From a narrative inquiry perspective, [research] can be emancipatory. You want to change the situation to something that is more equitable or something that is awake to world travelling or to the multiplicity of stories. But that does not necessarily mean it is your own practice or the practice of the people you have been studying. It is more about the transactional nature of sharing the experiences of your participants in a way of allowing that transaction to happen elsewhere. Not necessarily in that particular place where that particular study is happening. So I think when you get down to the beliefs and actions, you still want a social justification for the work. You want it and you want practical implications too. You don't want to do work that can't have practical implications [or applications]. But it's not necessarily for you in that situation or for the particular participants you are working with, even though I think that happens [as a result of the research]. So . . . that is one of the major differences between the methodologies related to action. I don't know if that makes sense to you Doug, or if you see autoethnography in a different way? I think that is one of the main differences between narrative inquiry and self-study of practice, and perhaps action research.

DOUG: I agree with those statements; [autoethnography] is that 'insider' account of a culture, for sure.

The point we believe should be emphasised here is that each of the four methodologies can and does provide practitioners with the frameworks and tools to help better understand the ways in which their beliefs and actions align. However, we came to a conclusion that each methodology often has a different focus or emphasis. For example, narrative inquiry and autoethnography both require the researcher to pay explicit attention to the beliefs (or values or histories) of research participants, including the practitioner researcher themselves. Writing about her autoethnographic process confronting entrenched racism, Carolyn Ellis stated: 'I wanted to show how/ why particular experiences have been challenging, important, and transformative; figure out how to live among racist others; and respond in a way that honoured my values by trying to value such racist wills. I wanted to turn my *insider* account toward larger, *outside* forces, considerations, and ways of living' (Adams, Holman Jones, & Ellis, 2015, p. 27). While researchers using autoethnographic approaches may include a focus on actions as Ellis did, they do not have to. Action research, on the other hand, does require the researcher to pay direct attention to action. Beliefs may not be given the same explicit attention as in narrative inquiry, for example, although as Ash implied, deciding a course of action automatically implicates beliefs (by choosing one course of action over another). However, those beliefs do not need to be a focus of the inquiry. Equally, by using the idea of the self-in-practice as an organising concept, self-study of practice *requires* the practitioner research to emphasise both beliefs *and* actions. John Loughran, one of the leading voices on self-study of practice research, stated this clearly, saying: 'an important aspect of self-study that is crucial in understanding this methodology is embedded in the desire of [practitioners] to better align their teaching intents with their teaching actions' (Loughran, 2007, p. 12).

As we continued exploring the nuances in each methodology's focus, we picked up on another concept that can help practitioner researchers understand what each approach offers and privileges. Specifically, we found that each methodology requires the practitioner researcher to have a different temporal focus; that is, there is a slightly different emphasis given to time periods. We turn our attention to this in the next section.

Each methodology has a distinct temporal focus

TIM: Doug, you said [earlier in the conversation] that autoethnography is past-referenced. I would say self-study of practice is future-oriented. One of LaBoskey's (2004) guidelines or criteria for quality in self-study of practice research is that it is aimed toward improvement. So the problem, or the research question, might be based on past experience but it is then researched moving forward. And so that is something that distinguishes self-study of practice further from autoethnography or perhaps narrative inquiry, I would say.

DOUG: From the autoethnographies I have read, most of them ended up getting to: 'Here is my study of my past, my culture, and here is the interaction of the individual in the culture' but not all of them have a future focus. Some do. It depends how it is written from the start. But I think that is a distinction for sure.

TIM: And I think it highlights a common misconception that some people have in wanting to do a self-study. Some might say: 'Well, I will just look at some of the things I did in the past and, hey presto, there is my self-study.' My response is: you might be looking at yourself but I don't know if that is a self-study of practice. It may be more suited to autoethnography or narrative inquiry.

LEE: And that is where a new conceptualisation of narrative inquiry-as-pedagogy is heading that a couple of us are writing about right now. I think that through studying and engaging with teachers and understanding their experiences, you can't help but have your pedagogy shift as a teacher educator [that is, if a teacher educator is studying teachers' practice]. I think narrative inquiry is past and present and also imagined. But I think some of the implications of being engaged in a methodology that asks you to do the things that narrative inquiry does, it can't help but affect your practice [in the future] in some way. Because you are now awake to it, it can help take you in that future-oriented direction in some ways. It's interesting you mention that: it wouldn't be the impetus [of most narrative inquiries] but from my experience of using it and watching my pedagogy as a university teacher shift, it definitely becomes future-oriented.

TIM: But it's not a necessity.

LEE: No, I don't think it's a necessity. But I think this is new in regards to being written about. As people begin to think about how their research is shaping their practice, I think the implications of using narrative inquiry is becoming more linked to shaping the pedagogy of the educational researcher.

ASH: There is an interesting thing from Lewin (1946). He talks about what happens now and what happens in the future, and it is the difference that you are interested in. So, from Lewin's perspective, there has to be an action; there has to be something that occurred. I think within an action research study, there is an action but I don't necessarily think that [applies to] autoethnography or narrative inquiry. In action research, there has to be an action at that time. There might be a future action as a consequence, or an acknowledgement of a current bias or of a current power situation.

DOUG: Yes, but at the same time, [focusing on something] that you just believe . . . well, you can't study that because it's ephemeral. It's just out there. I wrote in my notes that it might be helpful to think about autoethnography in the following way: beliefs in action = culture creation. Because when I take my beliefs as a classroom teacher and I put them into action, that creates a culture. Now I may not have expressed my beliefs accurately, so if I go back and look at that (although I'm not taking action at this point in time), I'm looking back at the beliefs in action and trying to understand if they were actually enacted.

ASH: OK, so there is an action but the action might be historical.

DOUG: Yes. And it could lead to future actions but it doesn't have to. I think if it is done well, then it will lead to future actions.

ASH: But what we are also saying is that [in autoethnography or narrative inquiry], it is enough to acknowledge how these beliefs were created and how that led to the creation of a culture [historically] . . . But in an action research study that would be a different kettle of fish. You wouldn't use an action research methodology to explore past actions. You would explore present actions. It would be about what you are doing and your present actions would inform how you change.

DOUG: However, your idea or research question, that might be based on looking at your past, mightn't it?

ASH: It may be. If we consider past-present-future, action research would mainly be concerned about the present and future. You may look at past. While autoethnography and narrative inquiry might be past and present but not necessarily future. So would self-study of practice then be past, present, and future?

TIM: Well, in order to arrive at your question in self-study of practice, you would have had to look into the past at some point, particularly regarding your beliefs, to ask: 'Well what is going on here that is causing me to question what I know and understand?'

ASH: But you have to investigate it, correct?

TIM: Yes. The focus of data collection and analysis would be how the self is engaging in practice in the present. So, it would be a study of the present through to the future.

ASH: It would have to be followed into the future?

TIM: Yes. If you thought about what you are interested in studying you might say: 'Well I came to this topic or issue because of some situations I have experienced'; however, that is just providing the context, it would not be the unit of analysis.

ASH: So in self-study of practice, practice has to be researched from present into future, even though you talk about past. Action research might not have past involved at all. It could simply be: 'This looks like a good idea and I am going to try to do it.'

Much like our discussion of the relative emphasis that might be given to beliefs and actions in the first section, we found certain considerations that need to be given to the temporal focus of the study when using each of the four methodologies. Specifically, we came to the conclusion that when using narrative inquiry and autoethnography, there is typically a focus on the past. That focus can be used to help understand what is going on in the present and in some cases to imagine what might occur in the future. Conversely, action research and self-study of practice tend to concentrate on the present with a firm eye to the future. While the past might inform the types of questions or approaches that are under investigation, the data collection takes place in the present and follows it through to the future.

These 'rules' do not mean that practitioner researchers using each of the four methodologies cannot delve into the past (using action research or self-study) or future (using narrative inquiry or autoethnography) for particular parts of the inquiry. However, when developing practitioner research questions, the temporal focus that the question implies might help the practitioner researcher decide which approach is best suited to their needs.

When raising the issue of research question development, we began thinking about who decides the research questions or focus in practitioner research. We delve into issues related to who decides on conducting practitioner research in the next section.

Who dictates the focus of practitioner inquiry?

TIM: Ash, can action research be dictated by an external authority? For example, could a school board require teachers to look at how they are implementing [a new set of] curriculum documents? [Because if they can], you might not necessarily have any deeply held beliefs that are being considered in that sort of inquiry.

ASH: Well, that is one of the big criticisms of action research. In the 1980s in the United States it became prescriptive. School boards were saying to practitioners: 'You will engage in action research'. The hunt for new [practitioner research] methodologies was due to a collapse in authenticity. It got devalued because it was imposed. Now I don't think modern day action research is about that. One of the reasons it got lambasted in the US [back then] was because it became a means of monitoring other people.

TIM: [Which might partially explain the development of self-study of practice]. One of self-study's key guidelines is that it is self-initiated and self-oriented (LaBoskey, 2004). So it is the individual practitioner who is identifying the phenomenon being investigated.

DOUG: I would say autoethnography is the same [as self-study of practice]. You would never have someone say: 'I want you to dive into your past'. No [external authority] is going to tell you something has to be self-initiated.

LEE: Interestingly I think the self-oriented emphasis is why teachers are so drawn to narrative inquiry. It's not about asking or telling you to make your practice better. In my opinion, it's more about asking ourselves what we might learn from the experiences of teachers who live in complex, ever changing professional knowledge landscapes. So it's not an intervention to see if we can take action and fix something, but more about how can we learn from you, and then, how might what we learn resonate, transact with others who read the work.

Among the reasons why people may want to learn more about conducting practitioner research is because they have to. As we found in our conversation, some practitioners are forced to engage in researching their practice as part of their professional responsibilities. Indeed, this is a prospect faced by teachers in the UK. For example, The Teachers' Standards (Department for Education, 2011, p. 7) state 'appropriate self-evaluation, reflection and professional development activity is critical to improving teachers' practice at all career stages'. This expectation is often formalised in teacher education courses with pre-service teachers engaging in action research projects – though, based on our explorations, these might actually take the form of autoethnographies, narrative inquiries, or self-studies of practice. However, this top-down approach to practitioner research and professional learning writ large has been found to be less effective than initiatives driven by practitioners themselves. That some 'new' forms of practitioner research, such as autoethnography and self-study of practice, begin with the practitioner researcher themselves – the challenges they are facing, the areas in which they want to improve – may partially explain why they have found a growing professional audience.

Conclusion

In this chapter we have explored the alignment of beliefs and actions as a common issue or dilemma well suited for exploration by practitioner researchers. Through our conversations, we considered the nuanced ways practitioner researchers might approach investigations that deal with the alignment of beliefs and actions when using each of the four methodologies explored in this book. In particular, we raised the following points as being important to acknowledge:

- the relative emphasis that practitioner researchers using each of the methodologies might give to beliefs and/or actions;
- the temporal focus each of the four methodologies privileges; and
- the role that practitioner researchers take when deciding on a practitioner research question or approach.

These are by no means the only points to consider when undertaking a practitioner research investigation that deals with the alignment of beliefs and actions, and we encourage practitioner researchers to identify other salient issues that inform what methodology is best suited to their needs, how the methodology will be used to frame and guide the practitioner research study, and what ideas and outcomes might be gleaned from the investigation.

References

Adams, T., Holman Jones, S., & Ellis, C. (2015). *Autoethnography: Understanding qualitative research*. New York: Oxford University Press.

Department for Education. (2011). *Teachers' standards: Guidance for school leaders, school staff, and governing bodies*. London: Department for Education. Retrieved 10 May 2017 from www.gov.uk/government/uploads/system/uploads/attachment_data/file/301107/Teachers__Standards.pdf.

LaBoskey, V.K. (2004). The methodology of self-study and its theoretical underpinnings. In J.J. Loughran, M.L. Hamilton, V.K. LaBoskey, and T. Russell (eds), *International handbook of self-study of teaching and teacher education practices* (pp. 817–869). Dordrecht: Kluwer Academic Press.

Lewin, K. (1946). Action research and minority problems. *Journal of Social Issues, 2*(4), 34–46.

Loughran, J. (2007). Researching teacher education practices: Responding to the challenges, demands, and expectations of self-study. *Journal of Teacher Education, 58*, 12–20.

PART V

As with all books, ours was reviewed by a number of colleagues (both academics and practitioners), and one of a number of useful suggestions around how we might improve the book, was to 'flip' the order of the first and last chapters. By repositioning the concluding chapter as the introductory chapter, we felt that we were better able to position the 'real-worldness' of practitioner researcher and offer an explanation and outline of the pressures that practitioners face as part of their roles, and offer solutions to help overcome these pressures, allowing for research to be conducted.

In doing this, we have been able to position practitioner research as something that is practical in nature. It has also allowed us, in this final section, to explore the thinking behind these methods. We felt, and still do, that now you have read the book you have a better idea of practitioner research. As such you are better prepared to explore these approaches in greater depth and look for new ways to extend their practice.

This section, therefore, provides an overview of practitioner research – both in the wider educational context and moving specifically to sport and physical education. Although we recognise that there is a significant part of the population that does not 'accept' practitioner research – especially the 'auto' varieties – we argue for its place and purpose within educational research.

13

OVERVIEW OF PRACTITIONER RESEARCH

Educational research

Throughout this book, we have explored four practitioner research methodologies, given examples of how they were used by Jo, Jodi, Brian and Ciara, respectively, and problematised issues of bias, ethics and the alignment of beliefs and actions. Throughout this process we've endeavoured to show that while there are characteristic differences between the separate methodologies, they share a common commitment to study personal practice with the view of improvement for the benefit of others (Dadds & Hart, 2001).

In our work, we have tried to present the reader with a sense of what it means to undertake practitioner research in physical education and youth sport. For postgraduate students (referred to as graduate students in North America) we have tried to provide examples and working practices that represent the rigour and robustness requested by academic supervisors and examiners while simultaneously presenting meaningful ways of researching your own practice in your professional context. For teachers and coaches, we have endeavoured to provide systematic ways of inquiring into and hopefully improving your practice in trustworthy and purposeful ways. In both cases, we have done so in the firm belief that undertaking practitioner research, in whatever form it takes, represents a strong commitment to meaningful and ongoing pedagogical and professional development. Above all, we have argued for the importance of practitioner research as professional learning and suggest:

1   Systematic study of one's own practice should be seen as an integral part of teaching physical education or coaching youth sport – inasmuch as practitioners should enact, model, and encourage this practice right from the start of their careers.

2   Increased recognition should be given to the need for action and inquiry, based on the idea that practitioners are fundamentally learners as well.
3   By embedding systematic study of one's own practice into early formal learning experiences (and seeing that modelled by supervising teachers/coaches or teacher/coach educators) such practice is more likely to become purposeful and habitual.
4   Systematic study of one's own practice should be seen as a way to foster professionalism on an ongoing basis throughout one's career and serve as a means of sustained professional development.

Practitioner research is not about building and then residing in an 'ivory tower', where one's work is detached from the reality of those for whom it is meant. It shouldn't be inaccessible, nor replete with long-winded, thesaurus juggling mumbo jumbo. It also shouldn't be deemed fit for purpose simply because it adheres to a set of scientific principles. It should be judged as research if it has the potential to have a meaningful impact on practice. If practical impact was a key factor in determining if 'something' should be considered research then, given the amount of research published in education, physical education and youth sport, what we see in schools and sports clubs should be a lot different to what we often witness. The truth is that a lot of research has little or no impact.

This is not a new problem. In preparing to write this final chapter we looked at a lot of 'old books' to see what they had to say – well, old inasmuch as they are about as old as we are (and that seemed as good a basis as any for defining them as old). Disappointingly, but probably not surprisingly, we found many of the same problems that we read and write about in our daily practice today. For example, in the preface to *Research for teachers* (a book first published in 1971), James Farrell reasoned that research must be usable if it is to be justified. He then identified three reasons why educational research wasn't usable: (1) teachers are unware of it, (2) researchers fail to communicate, and (3) teachers refuse to accept it (Farrell, 1971, p. ix).

Conversely, in the first edition of his seminal book *Conducting educational research* (which is now in its sixth edition), Tuckman (1972) argued that research involves the systematic formulation of generalisations based on the uncovering and interpretation of facts. This represents the traditional view of research. Such an argument reminds us of Stephen Corey's attempt to differentiate between research and action research. Writing in the late 1940s, Corey argued that 'the great majority of educational investigators are primarily interested in what I call fundamental or traditional research . . . their reports imply that they believe the primary purpose of educational research is to establish new generalizations stated as observed uniformities, explanatory principles, or scientific laws' (Corey, 1949, p. 509). In taking the minority position, Corey felt that action researchers (or practitioner researchers) have different purposes: ones that don't concern themselves with adding more truth but that focus on improving the educational practices in which they are engaged. Research is done in order to do a better job – to improve – and it is designed to affect actions. It is not about generalisations, but is about the particular learners, in the particular spaces, in the particular town or city in which the practitioner researcher works.

The problems identified by Corey in the 1940s were echoed several decades later by John Nisbet (the first president of the British Educational Research Association – founded in 1974). He suggested that while the foundations of educational research came from psychology with its preoccupation 'with measurement and statistical analysis' (Nisbet, 1980, p. 3), there was a move towards sociology and a diversification in the range of what counts for educational research. Drawing on the work of Michael Young in the mid-1960s, Nisbet (1980, pp. 5–6) highlighted the 'calamity of the gap between research and innovation' and argued that there is 'innovation without research – new ideas based on hunches, never tested objectively; and there is research without innovation – academic studies which make no impact and are unintelligible except to other researchers'. Practitioner research, in contrast, ensures that research 'monitors change, research is a guide to action, and the results of action are a guide to research' (ibid., p. 6).

As you can probably gather, the thrust of this problem is that different (and sometimes competing) notions of research exist. Historically and culturally, these differences tend to be located in knowledge disciplines, particularly between natural sciences and social sciences. The issue has trickled down and is particularly prominent in the field for which this book is aimed. In academic departments of sports science and kinesiology, there is often a distinction made between hard and soft science (similar to the distinction between natural and social science). This division also reflects a hierarchy, with the hard stuff of measurement, observation and 'objective' analysis of numbers being placed on a pedestal looking down upon softer notions of reflection, experience and the 'subjective' analysis of words and actions. In the section that follows, we apply a similar discussion to that which we have provided in the previous section, tracing the place of practitioner research in physical education and youth sport.

Does practitioner research have a place in physical education and youth sport?

Educational research is not alone in its adherence to measurement and statistics. In their *Introduction to research in health, physical education, recreation and dance* (HPERD), Thomas and Nelson (1985) presented the accepted research concepts, techniques and processes of undertaking research in HPERD. Specifically, they concentrated on four types of research: analytical, descriptive, experimental and creative (see Table 13.1).

Thomas and Nelson (ibid.) posited that research in HPERD can be viewed on a continuum with applied research and basic research at opposite extremes. They suggest that applied research addresses real world problems, conducted in real time and in real settings and often has a direct impact on practitioners. While this fits with our notions of practitioner research, they also suggest that there is a

TABLE 13.1 Types of research in health, physical education, recreation and dance.

Analytical	*Descriptive*	*Experimental*	*Creative*
Historical	Survey	Pre-designs	Choreography
Philosophical	Questionnaire	True designs	Sculpture
Reviews	Interview	Quasi-designs	Music
Meta-analysis	Normative		Art
	Case study		
	Job analysis		
	Documentary analysis		
	Developmental correlational		

great need to 'prepare proficient consumers and producers of research' (ibid., p. 6). The juxtaposing of 'consumers' and 'producers' speaks volumes of the fissure that lies between the two. Indeed, we suspect that Thomas and Nelson were suggesting teachers and coaches need to be prepared to consume rather than undertake research.

In addition to separating users and creators of research, Thomas and Nelson also define what they call 'quality' research efforts. They argue that such work would always involve some or all of the following:

> *identification* and delimitation *of a problem*; *searching, reviewing, and effectively writing about relevant literature*; specifying and defining testable hypotheses; designing the research to test the hypotheses; selecting, describing, testing, and treating the subjects; *analysing and reporting the results*; and *discussing the meaning and implications of the findings.*
>
> *(Thomas and Nelson, 1985, p. 6; emphasis added)*

From their argument, we believe that practitioner research would actively involve the passages we have italicised. That is: *identification of a problem*; *searching, reviewing, and effectively writing about relevant literature*; *analysing and reporting the results*; and *discussing the meaning and implications of the findings.* While there is value in conducting research that involves hypotheses and so on, much of the research we have conducted along with many colleagues (as practitioner researchers or otherwise) has not included these processes. Yet, traditional views of research, such as those proposed by Thomas and Nelson more than thirty years ago, are still privileged in the diverse world of physical education and sport research today.

Since 2000 there have been, we believe, three key texts published that represent compilations of major themes, innovations and/or trends in physical education and youth sport; each of which is relevant to our discussion about the place of practitioner research in our field. We will discuss these and consider the place of practitioner research in those texts.

The *Handbook of physical education* (Kirk, Macdonald, & O'Sullivan, 2006) represents one of the most comprehensive efforts to bring together much of the research that had been conducted in physical education (and to a lesser extent, coach education) up to the time of publication. It included 45 chapters (800+ pages) contributed by over 50 authors who are considered to be leaders in the field. *Research methods in physical education and youth sport* (Armour & Macdonald, 2012) is an important and innovative contribution that provides readers with an introduction to some of the ways to conduct research in our field. Again, it is quite extensive, comprising 26 chapters from around 50 authors. These books were followed by the recent publication of the *Routledge handbook of physical education pedagogies* (Ennis, 2017), which consists of 44 chapters contributed by approximately 70 authors. To make some simplistic observations of the place of practitioner research in these books, here are the combined number of index entries for some key terms we have used in this book: practitioner research (0), practitioner researcher (0), teacher research (1), action research (2), narrative inquiry (3), autoethnography (6) and self-study (1).

While this summary might be disappointing (but not surprising) to some readers, it masks some good news, which is the inclusion of several chapters on topics similar to those discussed in this book. For example, in the first handbook is a chapter by Armour (2006) titled 'The way to a teacher's heart: Narrative research in physical education'. In that chapter, Armour frames her discussion in terms of narrative research (which should not be confused with narrative inquiry as we explained in Chapter 3). She states that regardless of the specific research methodology that is being used, her aim was to review research where there was 'a fundamental concern with using narrative techniques to encourage personal analysis, critical understanding and, where warranted, pedagogical change' (ibid., p. 467). We find that to a great extent, our intentions in this book mirror those explained by Armour, highlighting the value of practitioner research for the practitioner themselves and for the learners with whom they are working alongside. She also emphasises the need to position research in such a way as to make it engaging for practitioners rather than as 'a sterile, detached activity conducted largely for the benefit of other academic researchers' (ibid., p. 468).

While the content of the chapter is excellent, what is somewhat discouraging is the number of studies Armour (ibid.) was able to review that fell under the banner of practitioner research or research using narrative methods (we estimate from the reference list around 25–30). We assume that one reason for the relatively small number of studies published is because of academic researchers' views on the quality and place of practitioner research in physical education research outlets, such as conferences and journals. Because the vast majority of research submitted to journals is reviewed by researchers in the field through the peer review process, the definition or view of research that peer reviewers bring with them to their reading is crucial in their judgment of what counts as quality in the research being reviewed. In many cases, all it takes for research not to be accepted is for a reviewer to say something like: 'This is overly biased and therefore invalid because it is written by the person whose practice was being examined' or 'Because the results are not generalisable this does not represent a significant contribution to our knowledge of physical education or youth sport'. Over time, many editors and reviewers have become sympathetic, open and even encouraging of practitioner research proposals. Yet we feel there still remains, in many cases, an underlying need to argue for and convince readers of the value of practitioner research rather than assume they hold the position from the outset.

As an example, consider the following interaction one of us encountered from a submission of practitioner research to an eminent journal in our field in the past ten years. In offering the opinion that the paper should be rejected, one reviewer said:

> The study contained several problems that bring into question the quality of the data. First, the teacher in this study was the lead author, who then wrote reflective statements and quoted him/herself in the findings! There is no way to independently verify those statements.

A reviewer for the same journal, in the last four years, rejected another practitioner research paper, in part, due to the methodology of choice:

> My third, and most problematic series of questions comes from the use of a teacher–researcher in a validation/reliability study of this kind. My concerns became compounded as I read the several self-quotes in the qualitative section of the results. The authors' attempts to eliminate bias actually raised more serious questions for me.

This experience is similar to that described by Holt (2003), who discusses and critiques reviewers' comments from an autoethnographic study on his experience as an early PhD student and athlete. He reconstructs feedback from reviewers regarding their perceptions of the rigour, value and principles of autoethnography in relation to 'necessary qualities' of scientific research.

Interestingly, when Bullough and Pinnegar (2001) published their ground-breaking piece 'Guidelines for quality in autobiographical forms of self-study research' in the prestigious journal *Educational Researcher*, a primary reason for its publication was because of its controversy, originality and the way it rejected many traditional research practices as much as it was for the quality of scholarship. The editor at the time made an executive decision to publish the article because of the new directions it took educational research, despite the recommendations of *seven* reviewers that the work not be published (S. Pinnegar, personal communication, 9 June 2017). It endures as a highly cited work in the field of qualitative research in education and an essential piece of reading for those interested in autobiographical forms of inquiry.

The plain fact is, practitioner research – particularly when it is couched in autobiography – has its fierce opponents and practitioner researchers begin the publication process with many more obstacles and assumptions than researchers whose work might be described as traditional.

In the research methods text (Armour & Macdonald, 2012), there are two chapters of particular relevance and interest to practitioner researchers. Armour and Chen (2012) contributed a chapter on narrative research methods (again with a broad focus on narrative research and including but not limited to narrative inquiry and autoethnography) while Rossi and Tan (2012) authored a chapter on action research. The focus of these chapters was very different to the chapters in the Handbook (Kirk et al., 2006) because the authors aimed to explain how the methodologies and methods worked and could/should be used. Like our book, the overarching purpose was more along the lines of 'how to' rather than 'what has been done'. With that said, the inclusion of these two chapters signifies some recognition of the value of these types of research, not only for practitioners but for beginning researchers generally and for the broader research community (of practitioners, academics, policy makers, and so on).

In the most recent handbook (Ennis, 2017) some consideration is also given to concepts we have expressed as being relevant for practitioner researchers. The chapter on 'Interpretive and critical research' (Woods & Graber, 2017) recognises several examples of narrative research and self-study, explaining what they represent for the field. The chapter on narrative inquiry (Dowling & Garrett, 2017) provides a deep discussion of the history of narrative inquiry and its presence in physical education research and stands as one of the few examples to go into great depth about its history and future in the field. However, most of the discussion within the handbook focuses broadly on methodologies appropriate for practitioner research rather than on practitioner research *per se*. That is, there is limited attention paid to unpacking examples of practitioner research, what they represent and what they contribute to the field.

What we might take from this summary is that the methodologies we have deemed useful for practitioners (action research, narrative inquiry, autoethnography and self-study of practice) are being recognised as valuable in the field of physical education and youth sport. And while some examples of practitioner research are having a degree of impact (e.g. Attard & Armour, 2005; Casey, Dyson, & Campbell, 2009) in terms of readership and citations, we are not entirely convinced that the research community values practitioner research as standing alongside other (arguably more widely accepted) forms of research. The message we believe this sends to practitioners is that researchers cannot or are not willing to learn from experiences of practice in ways that value the practitioner's voice, experience and insight. In the following section, we articulate ways in which we have learned from the research conducted by the practitioners we worked with in Part III of the book.

As researchers, what have we learned from the practitioners?

The dominant story of research is that others can learn from it. Of course, we hope that practitioners and researchers alike pick up this book, use it, learn from it, critique it, and so on. We mostly hope that whoever reads this book finds it to be practical, applicable and useful in regard to their practice or their research. However, if we only saw this work as singular in its purpose – to help others – perhaps we could be seen as hypocrites or worse; as researchers who are moving their careers forwards on the backs of practitioners.

Truthfully, we hope that this book illustrates how much we have learned from working alongside Jo, Jodi, Brian and Ciara individually and collectively. Not just about the research process, but about their practice, their students, their struggles and in turn how that relates to our own work as researchers and as teacher educators. In many ways, this book became a professional development project for each of us. We found ourselves excited to discuss the unfolding chapters, methodological dilemmas and critical questions surrounding who would find this work useful. As relationships became stronger, it became clear that we were much more comfortable telling someone if they were out to lunch. Some of the Skype conversations lasted hours and we still had plenty to discuss when we disconnected. Even though the practitioners were not involved in person during these conversations, the ways they pushed us to think often became one of the richest parts of our dialogue.

While it may seem as though we argue for more practitioner research to improve the practice of teachers, we also make an argument for more practitioner research to improve the practice of teacher educators and other researchers. Providing practitioners with a venue to translate their knowledge to the field, as Armour (2006) argued, is just as important as researchers critiquing practice.

What we learned from the book

Ash: For those who are fans of *Game of Thrones*, the term 'you know nothing Jon Snow' will have powerful connotations. For those who haven't read or watched *Game of Thrones*, then I will explain. Jon Snow is beyond the wall, he is leading a wildling captive, Ygritte, and despite her bonds she likes to inform him of his ignorance – an ignorance he can't yet see. And she is right. He is walking in the wrong direction, is being followed and is soon overpowered by her brethren and the captor becomes the captive. This, for me, was the key message from the book. I know nothing. Well, very little. In working with Tim, Lee and Doug I quickly came to realise this and when working with Jo I was challenged in so many ways. When I had the chance to read Jodi, Brian and Ciara's work I was humbled. There should be no taken for granted truths or 'givens' when it comes to pedagogy and pedagogues. Schools are the same and they shouldn't be bunched together. From such arrogance come ignorance. And we are left knowing nothing and yet pretending to know everything. I am not an expert but just someone who understands my reality a little better than you. Perhaps?!

Lee: This book re-affirmed for me how difficult it can be to do collaborative work. Especially with people across the country, time zones and an ocean. It also re-affirmed that the aspects of our lives that are most difficult, are oftentimes the most rewarding. As researchers I think it can become comforting to stick with what we know, in our own little silos. I am convinced, now more than ever, that this is the easiest thing to do. But I have to say that writing with three colleagues from different contexts, with different perspectives, beliefs and different methodologies, was one of the most rewarding professional experiences I have had. Being pushed out of my comfort zone, and out of my silo, demonstrated how much there is to learn when we become awake to other ways of knowing and understanding. I was also reminded often how privileged, perhaps lucky, I am to be able to work with amazing scholars and practitioners across the world who have the same passions about physical education, research, and teaching.

Doug: A long time teacher friend of mine first introduced me to the saying, 'faster alone, further together'. That statement epitomises this book. Faster is not always better and we have come very, very far (OK, I have come very, very far) in many ways. Ash, Tim and Lee have critiqued, pushed and challenged me – ultimately making me a better scholar and teacher–educator. We laughed a lot, worked pretty damn hard and lived the phrase, 'iron sharpens iron'. Working with Jodi and reading the work of Jo, Brian and Ciara has been much more than rewarding and enlightening. It has reminded me of the fundamental importance of listening to and working closely with those who are 'in it' – daily. Their journeys and purposeful focus humble and inspire me. As a researcher and teacher–educator I can't emphasise enough the impact of practitioner research on what I am knowing and who I am becoming.

Tim: When I am writing up one of my self-study research projects, I am always conscious of the ways in which autobiographical forms of research can be interpreted as navel gazing or a means to self-justification. I get the critique. What stood out to me from reading across the pieces by Jo, Brian, Jodi and Ciara and from working with Ash, Lee and Doug was the ways in which their respective approaches to practitioner research represented not just a commitment to self-improvement, they represented a commitment to improve the experiences of the young people (in the case of Jo, Brian, Jodi and Ciara) or the teachers they work with (in the case of Ash, Lee and Doug). Regardless of the methodology that was used or being advocated for, or whether the person was looking into the past, present or future, all of them stood as very strong examples of wanting to do what is best for their students or athletes. Practitioner research often includes 'I' or 'we' a lot (as in 'I/we did this' or 'I/we found that') and sometimes this masks the real nub of the issue being explored: 'them' or 'they' ('they really responded well to the new approach' or 'I was not challenging them enough and something had to change'). Readers do not need to do much digging in the chapters to recognise the unflinching commitment the practitioners have to young people. And so while using the first person is almost required in writing up or sharing a piece of practitioner research, the examples provided show that the real reason most practitioners' inquiries are begun in the first place is because of the people the 'I/we' is working with.

References

Armour, K. (2006). The way to a teacher's heart: Narrative research in physical education. In D. Kirk, D., Macdonald & M. O'Sullivan (eds), *The handbook of physical education* (pp. 467–485). Thousand Oaks, CA: Sage.

Armour, K., & Chen, H.H. (2012). Narrative research methods. In K. Armour & D. Macdonald (eds), *Research methods in physical education and youth sport* (pp. 237–249). Abingdon: Routledge.

Armour, K., & MacDonald, D. (eds). (2012). *Research methods in physical education and youth sport*. Abingdon: Routledge.

Attard, K., & Armour, K.M. (2005). Learning to become a learning professional: Reflections on one year of teaching. *European Journal of Teacher Education*, *28*(2), 195–207.

Bullough Jr, R.V., & Pinnegar, S. (2001). Guidelines for quality in autobiographical forms of self-study research. *Educational Researcher*, *30*(3), 13–21.

Casey, A., Dyson, B., & Campbell, A. (2009). Action research in physical education: Focusing beyond myself through cooperative learning. *Educational Action Research*, *17*(3), 407–423.

Corey, S.M. (1949). Curriculum development through action research. *Educational Leadership*, *7*, 147–153.

Dadds, M., & Hart, S. (2001). *Doing practitioner research differently*. London: Routledge.

Dowling, F., & Garrett, R. (2017). The transformative possibilities of narrative inquiry. In C.D. Ennis (ed.), *Routledge handbook of physical education pedagogies* (pp. 332–342). Abingdon: Routledge.

Ennis, C.D. (ed.). (2016). *Routledge handbook of physical education pedagogies*. Abingdon: Routledge.

Farrell, J.B. (1971). *Research for teachers*. Sydney: Angus & Roberson.

Holt, N.L. (2003). Representation, legitimation, and autoethnography: An autoethnographic writing story. *International journal of qualitative methods*, *2*(1), 18–28.

Kirk, D., MacDonald, D., & O'Sullivan, M. (eds). (2006). *Handbook of physical education*. Thousand Oaks, CA: Sage.

Nisbet, J. (1980). Educational Research: The state of the art. In W.B. Dockrell & D. Hamilton (eds), *Rethinking Educational Research* (pp. 1–10). London: Hodder & Stoughton.

Rossi, A., & Tan, W.K. (2012). Action research in physical education: cycles, not circles! In. K. Armour & D. Macdonald (eds), *Research methods in physical education and youth sport* (pp. 250–262). Abingdon: Routledge.

Thomas, J.R., & Nelson, J.K. (1985). *Introduction to research in health, physical education, recreation, and dance*. Champaign, IL: Human Kinetics.

Tuckman, B.W. (1972). *Conducting educational research*. New York: Harcourt, Brace, Jovanovich.

Woods, A.M., & Graber, K.C. (2017). Interpretive and critical research: A view through a qualitative lens. In C.D. Ennis (ed.), *Routledge handbook of physical education pedagogies* (pp. 21–33). Abingdon: Routledge.

INDEX